RETENTION STRATEGIES

The key to attracting and
retaining excellent employees

Dr Mark Bussin

TALENT MANAGEMENT SERIES

First published in 2018.

ISBN: 978-1-86922-767-8
eISBN: 978-1-86922-768-5 (PDF ebook)

Published by KR Publishing
P O Box 3954
Randburg
2125
Republic of South Africa

Tel: (011) 706-6009
Fax: (011) 706-1127
E-mail: orders@knowres.co.za
Website: www.kr.co.za

Printed and bound: HartWood Digital Printing, 243 Alexandra Avenue, Halfway House, Midrand
Typesetting, layout and design: Cia Joubert, cia@knowres.co.za
Cover design: Marlene de'Lorme, marlene@knowres.co.za
Editing and proofreading: Jennifer Renton, jenniferrenton@live.co.za
Project management: Cia Joubert, cia@knowres.co.za

Table Of Contents

About the Author

Dr Mark Bussin

Mark is the Chairperson of 21st Century, a specialist reward and remuneration consultancy. He has HR, reward and remuneration experience across all industry sectors, and is viewed as a thought leader in the HR, reward and remuneration arena. He serves on and advises numerous Boards and Remuneration Committees on Executive Remuneration. Mark holds a Doctorate in Commerce. He has published or presented over 350 articles and papers, and has received awards for his outstanding articles in this field. He has appeared on television and radio, and in the press, giving his expert views on remuneration. Mark is a guest lecturer at several universities and supervises Masters' and Doctoral theses in the Reward area. He is a past President of SARA (South African Reward Association) and a past Commissioner for the remuneration of Public Office-Bearers in the Presidency. Mark tutors reward and finance modules for WorldatWork globally.

Mark enjoys flying Cessnas and loves his family time.

Mark can be contacted at drbussin@mweb.co.za or +27829010055, or visit his website: www.drbussin.com.

Books written by Prof Bussin:

Bussin, M. (2012). *The Performance Management for Emerging Markets.* Randburg: Knowres Publishing.
Bussin, M. (2013). *Performance Management for Government, Universities, Schools and NGOs.* Randburg: Knowres Publishing.
Bussin, M. (2014). *Remuneration and Talent Management.* Randburg: Knowres Publishing
Bussin, M. (2015). *Expatriate Compensation.* Bryanston: Knowres Publishing.
Bussin, M. (2017). *Performance Management REBOOT: Fresh perspectives for the changing world of work.* Bryanston: Knowres Publishing.

Introduction

Who is this book for?

This book is for anyone who manages or leads people currently, or will lead them in the future. How to ensure that people want to work for you, follow you and stay with you willingly is covered in this book. Staying with one employer for a very long time is now passé. Today's trend is to work with an employer and grow your CV. Work needs to be stretching and interesting; if my CV is not growing, I will leave and line managers need to be aware of that. This book is also intended for HR and Reward executives, who are often responsible for crafting policy involving employment. Our policies are in need of a total refresh and this book may provide you with some ideas on what to include and exclude.

Using this book

Chapter 1 covers the business case for retention strategies and the costs and implications of unwanted high staff turnover. Whilst reward is touched on in the chapter one, **Chapter 2** unpacks the role of rewards and remuneration. I have always thought that remuneration only accounts for 25% of the stay decision, but that it is a ticket to the retention game – it just has to be fair. **Chapter 3** covers retention and engagement and they are intertwined. Whilst engagement does not necessarily cause retention, there is some relationship. How to keep employees engaged is unpacked in this chapter. **Chapter 4** covers remuneration options for retention and how each is typically used in organisations. This assumes that we have ticked all the other retention boxes like interesting work and great leadership.
Chapter 5 covers the Employee Value Proposition (EVP) and its linkage to retention and remuneration. Lastly, **Chapter 6** covers the retention of different generations.

Chapter 1

The business case for retention strategies

This chapter covers:

- Why retention strategies are necessary in the world of work – or retention as a risk mitigation against an unpredictable world of work.
- How poor retention impacts the workplace and employees.
- Why people leave an organisation.
- Why it is important to keep them.
- The taxonomy of retention.
- Retention interventions.

Retention as a strategy in an increasingly dynamic world

"Turbulent", "competitive", "unstable", "unpredictable" - these are the key words that summarise the business world we are involved in today. The parallel most important key word is "retention".

Having received the desired training, knowledge, skills and abilities, it is exceedingly common for individuals to switch to different organisations for a more lucrative salary and more desirable working environment, with more suitable work times, growth prospects and other such temptations. With the threat of an employee moving on, management and the Human Resources (HR) team are responsible for immediate intervention as well uncovering the motivation preceding the decision to leave. But even before that, strategies of retention tailored to the particular workplace must be put in place to ensure that top talent stays with the organisation.

Checklist – Analyse your workplace

Select your workplace/a particular business unit/ an area in your workplace and create a summary of employee movements and perceptions of factors impacting why employees have left or why they choose to stay.

Why do people leave?	Why do people stay?
Analyse the data from the last two years to try assess how many people have left and why. This exercise could take some time – you should use employee exit data, exit interviews, managers' reports, and even follow-up interviews with people who have already left. *Employees who have been out of an organisation for some time are often more open to discussing their perceptions openly and candidly.* *Also include people who have expressed an interest in leaving – who are they, what are their reasons? Are they push reasons or pull reasons? In other words, is something negative pushing them out, or is something positive from the external environment pulling them in?*	*Often, when people analyse the workplace, the factors causing employees to leave are emphasised and management tries to stop them leaving. This often results in top talent being incentivised to stay with external motivations like a salary increase or title change. But this is only the tip of the iceberg of what makes people stay or feel loyal to an organisation.* *To assess what makes them stay, ask people in the organisation what they value about the organisation, what makes them stay, what makes them loyal, and what stops them moving to a competitor.*

What is retention, and why is it important?

Employee retention can be summarised as the process through which employees are encouraged to remain in an organisation for as long as possible. In the current economic environment, it is one of the foremost concerns of all organisations. All over the world, increasing attention is being paid to how to drive retention. There are multiple conferences addressing retention; leading organisations are citing retention as a key challenge and central objective; and no organisation can expect to survive if its retention game is not on point.

Fact: Recruiters place employee retention and employee quality as a top priority.

Retention is, in fact, a win-win deal for both parties – the employer and the employee. The employer scratches their employee's back by offering them dreams, such as a supportive working environment, a healthy lifestyle, as well as reward and recognition. The employee reciprocates by scratching their employer's back by means of saved expenses for the organisation – recruitment, selection and training costs are all averted if employees do not leave. These factors will be discussed in detail further on.

In essence, retention leads to lower turnover rates. Turnover leads to:

- costs to the company in terms of lower revenues and profitability;
- impact to employees in terms of greater workload and lower productivity, possibly leading to more turnover; and
- reduced employee morale as a result of greater workloads and the perception that the organisation does not value strategies to retain people.

A high turnover rate occurs when a company loses a high percentage of employees in relation to the number of people hired. This implies that the company lacks sufficient retention strategies to function effectively. It is crucial for any organisation to have an effective retention strategy in place to control employee turnover and keep the organisation functioning at the optimum level.

Summary of main points

To sum up, high turnover levels are undesirable as they cause:

- poor performance;
- low morale;
- client confusion and a lack of continuity;
- compromised productivity; and
- a loss of revenue as a result of decreased sales.

Why do people leave an organisation?

Why are retention strategies in such high demand? Why the increased focus from management research and workplace training on retention? Why not focus on greater productivity, better team work, or even leadership skills? The simple answer is that all of these factors are just sub-factors of retention. In fact, research shows that employees primarily leave organisations for the reasons listed below. (As you go through the reasons, consider if you have experienced any of these personally or if you know others in your organisation who are experiencing them now.)

	✓
Constant friction with peers or superiors - Let's face it, no one wants to be stuck in a negative working environment where constant confrontation occurs or there is a constant digression in viewpoints. This can be taxing for the employee and result in unhappiness.	
Undesirable remuneration - A salary that is too low can result in feelings of discrimination by the employee. Everyone likes to believe that they are valued and that the effort they put in is fairly rewarded.	
Little room for growth - A lack of career development or advancement can result in feelings of stagnation. Everyone needs a "change" in life, or the opportunity to grow. Employees who feel "stuck" will seek advancement opportunities elsewhere.	
Lack of motivation - Work that lacks meaning or value to an employee, such as menial or monotonous tasks that do not challenge them, results in the loss of motivation for the employee. This will lead them to seek work elsewhere that will be more fulfilling to them.	
Pregnancy and family requirements - Family comes first if a good enough deal is not put on the table to manage family and a job.	
Clash of values - It sometimes happens that the values of the organisation do not match the personality or values of the employee.	
Lack of engagement - Employee engagement and retention are two parts of the same process; a disengaged employee is at serious risk of leaving an organisation.	

Retention myths and truths

The table below sets out some of the fundamentals when it comes to truths and myths regarding retention.

Table 1: Truths and myths about retention

Myth	Truth
Money is the reason people leave Money definitely does play a pivotal role in an employee's decision to leave a company, and low pay will certainly result in perceptions of unfairness. However, if an employee is being paid on a par with the competitive market level, other aspects of the way they are treated by the organisation will impact their decision to leave.	**The key to keep talent is to offer an environment where they can grow and thrive** An environment that encourages and supports employees is great. It is not the only prerequisite of talent retention, but it is certainly one of the key factors.
Hiring and retention are not correlated In fact, hiring and retention have a strong correlation. It is important to recruit and select people who are fitting for the job as well as being the most likely to be loyal to the company. Selecting individuals with the right job and organisational fit increases retention.	**Retention should be a major focal point when undergoing organisational change** Organisational change specifically dictates a time to be concerned about retention. Organisational factors may determine who stays or leaves the company; it is a common time for valued employees whom the company intended to stay, to choose to leave. Often, mergers or acquisitions leave employees insecure about job security and the future of the organisation and their employment.

Myth	Truth
Training merely means you are training them for another employer	**Regardless of outcome, training is necessary**
An organisation may decide that its employees have sufficient knowledge, skills and abilities to perform the requirements of their jobs. They may see training as an unnecessary expense that will only benefit employees if they choose to leave.	CFO to CEO: What if we train our employees and they leave? CEO to CFO: What if we don't, and they stay?

CASE STUDY

Maternity benefits and retention

While some women in male-dominated occupations may display masculine characteristics in order to integrate successfully, it is essential to acknowledge the feminine biological and social roles of women outside of their work environment.[1] An important consideration in the recruitment of women is the fact that some women are primarily responsible for family responsibilities, which include pregnancy and child care.

But why focus on re-hiring when you can just retain?
Maternity benefits curtail post-maternity attrition of women employees
One of the major reasons behind the failed retention of women is pregnancy. People prioritise their families over jobs, so when the time comes to make a decision, family will come first. For this reason, organisations need to help by providing women with support which makes it easier and more enticing for them to remain with the organisation. Maternity benefits are one of the principal retention strategies for female employees. Countries such as India protect the rights of female individuals by means of law; India's Maternity Benefit Act (1961) protects the rights of women and the benefits they are entitled to, such as compulsory maternity leave with salary and flexi-work post maternity leave.

In India, several organisations have over the last few years introduced new policies to curtail attrition among women employees post maternity leave. Between 2003 and 2010, according to Avtar[2], a diversity and inclusion consulting firm, over 48% of employed women under 30 years of age dropped out of the workforce due to maternity and childcare. This is a challenge that Indian organisations are facing head-on. From flexi-work to phase back programmes, no stone has been left unturned, and the hard work is finally paying off. Organisations are witnessing a gradual reduction in attrition levels among women employees post maternity leave.

Maersk Group India saw a steady increase in attrition among women employees post maternity, from 3% in 2013 to 7% in 2016. IBM India, on the other hand, reduced attrition among women employees by 10% in two years, while at Cummins, a return-to-work programme called 'Reboot', which was launched in May 2016, has already seen a positive outcome.

In April 2016, Maersk introduced improved maternity benefits of a minimum 18 weeks of maternity leave on full pay, as well as a phased return-to-work programme with reduced hours by 20% on full pay for up to six months to all employees who return from maternity leave. Year on year, 3% to 5% of its female workforce go on maternity leave. Maersk realised that when women return to their careers, they may sense reduced confidence levels, and many lose leadership roles to their peers who remained in the workforce. It was thus critical for Maersk, which has a women-to-men workforce ratio of 30:70, to introduce a 'return-to-work' initiative and transition employees from a career break to full-time careers. Women leaders are provided with real-time challenging business project opportunities, which are deployed through a holistic orientation and developmental programme focusing on specific skills and capabilities, to encourage them to settle in their roles as soon as possible, with the help of an assigned mentor.

Standard Chartered Bank was among the first companies to offer six months maternity leave, which was soon copied by many other companies, but even after offering the best-in-class six months, the attrition rate of women who went on maternity leave was high, at 35-40%. Most returning mothers were plagued with guilt and in spite of having very understanding managers, they decided to drop out.

Read more at:
http://economictimes.indiatimes.com/articleshow/56289061.cms?utm_source=contentofinterest&utm_medium=text&utm_campaign=cppst

Why then, is it so important to retain employees?

There are a number of reasons to retain employees. Eight of these will now be discussed in more detail.

Eight reasons to retain employees

1. The **cost** incurred to organisations - statistics show that the replacement of lost talent costs the company between 70% and 200% of that employee's annual salary. Costs are typically incurred from advertising, recruitment procedures, selection procedures, training and other such organisational operations. The retention of employees thus allows the organisation to suppress overall costs.

2. **Competition** - after an employee leaves an organisation, they return to the job market. This is unfavourable for the organisation left behind as it has allocated ample resources and time to developing the employee who often goes to work for a competitor organisation. These employees take their acquired knowledge, skills and abilities and apply them to the new organisation, leaving the previous organisation a step behind. Furthermore, an organisational successor may be lost, leaving the organisation with the burden of building a new talent pipeline according to the organisation's needs.

3. **Time lost** - once a new employee is hired, both time and resources need to be allocated to assist the new hire to learn the ways of the organisation. Time and training is therefore reallocated to the employee as opposed to focusing on clients and the overall organisational objectives. Furthermore, time is needed for each individual to understand and adjust to others. One needs to acclimatise to one's team members to be comfortable with them, to understand them, to trust them, and eventually to rely on them and reciprocate thereafter. When a team member is replaced, time is needed to rebuild this type of relationship.

4. **An affected client base** - an organisation's success largely depends on client satisfaction, loyalty and customer perception. An organisation therefore holds its reputation at stake when the turnover rate is high, due to the clientele having bad perceptions of the organisation. By the same token, the employee leaving the organisation might take clients with them, which will result in a loss of clients and revenue for the organisation.

5. **Effect on work culture** - employees who work at the same organisation for a long period of time pick up traits from each other in due course. The tendency of adopting positive qualities from one another is commonplace, allowing co-workers to be so in sync that tasks are completed more hastily and efficiently.

6. **Employee adaptability** - employees who work for an organisation for a long period of time have strong familiarity with the policies and practices of the company, therefore they are able to adjust better to the job demands than individuals who change jobs more frequently. Those individuals who know their organisations like the back of their hand thus have the ability to contribute in the most effective manner, leading their companies to function more efficiently.

7. **Loyalty** - individuals who remain at an organisation for longer are more loyal to both the company and the management thereof. Due to the benefits they have received from the organisation, they become more attached. Deviant behaviours, such as slacking at work, petty theft or bad mouthing the organisation is a rarity. They treat the organisation as a family member, and think and speak of it fondly.

8. **Talent is the backbone of the organisation** - innovative, hard-working, talented employees who can think out the box are what allow the organisation to remain competitive. Without these employees, the organisation would suffer. Key talent is difficult to source, thus when it is, it is important to retain.

Employees are the building blocks of each and every organisation. They carry out the day-to-day operations of the organisation, performing the necessary tasks and maintaining the necessary relationships. No organisation can function efficiently without its dedicated, hard-working employees; an incredible amount of time and resources are allocated to recruiting these employees, and just as much effort needs to be allocated to retaining them. For this reason, every organisation should have retention strategies in place.

tips/ideas

Tip: Employees who stay at an organisation the longest are those who are treated well by their employers. Organisations based upon loyalty are admired by others and perceived more favourably.

An important means by which the employer can contribute to the positive treatment of their employees is by getting to know each individual on a personal basis. Employees will feel valued as well as more comfortable in the work environment, which will positively affect retention rates.

The following TED Talk video highlights the importance of putting employees first. This will have a positive impact on your organisation: https://www.youtube.com/watch?v=hvcOzkK2rcg

The business impact of retention

The impact of staff turnover on business is significant, thus the concepts of engagement and the Employee Value Proposition (EVP) are essential to consider. Successful organisations continually try to improve their attractiveness to employees and spend time asking their employees what would make them stay and how to make it more attractive to work at the company. Some concepts are defined below:

Retention can be defined as an organisation's ability "to hold and keep in possession and to engage the services of high potentials (HIPOs) and value contributors in mission critical and scarce skills positions".[3]

Engagement is key to effective retention as it is "the state in which individuals are emotionally and intellectually committed to the organisation or group".

Commitment is another critical factor as it drives performance and retention. It has both an emotional component - the extent to which employees value, enjoy, and believe in their organisation, as well as a rational component - the extent to which employees believe it is in their best interests to stay with the organisation.

Research has consistently demonstrated that **engagement** and **commitment** are both vital ingredients in effective **retention** strategies. A Watson Wyatt study[4] found that a company with highly engaged employees achieved a financial performance four times greater than companies with poor engagement. It also found strong correlations between the highly engaged and top performers, as well as with healthy staff (fewer days off for illness). Development Dimension International (DDI)[5] found that turnover in low engagement teams averaged 14.5% compared with 4.8% in highly engaged teams.

---

tips/ideas

Tip: Adapt your strategies according to your audience. In other words, there is no one-size-fits-all; the principles may be the same, but a workplace has special characteristics that must be kept in mind.

An **EVP** also plays a significant role in attracting employees and building commitment. An effective EVP provides organisations with three quantifiable benefits:

- Improved attractiveness - source from a much deeper pool of talent (up to 20% more), including passive talent (those who are not actively seeking other opportunities).

- Greater employee commitment - significantly higher employee commitment levels. Up to 40% of the workforce displays high levels of commitment, as opposed to less than 10% in under-performing organisations.

- Remuneration savings - reduce the remuneration premium required to attract new candidates and spend 10% less on base pay compared to under-performing organisations.

What is it that people are searching for?

Now that we have discussed how organisations suffer from employee turnover as well as what employees *do not* want, it is time to discuss what they do want. How do we develop an effective retention strategy to keep employees happy, motivated and retained? First, we need to make peace with the fact that a certain percentage of employees want to move regardless. They have their own reasons and it is costly to restrain them.

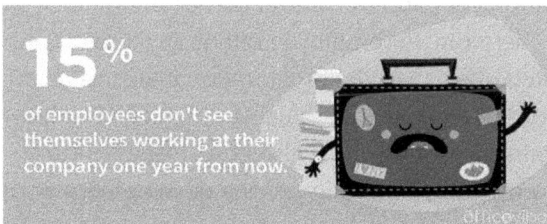

15% of employees don't see themselves working at their company one year from now.

The following is a guide to developing the most effective retention strategy for your organisation:

1. *Hire the right people from the beginning*

    From the beginning, an interview can provide you with knowledge regarding whether an individual is the best fit for your organisation. Hiring the best fit will reveal how to retain them without losing time on creating an effective employee retention strategy. Restrain from asking textbook questions within the interview. Cover their motivations, their accomplishments, the reason they applied for the job, how their weaknesses impact their work, and the likes.

     See this TED Talk by Jack Ma – the Founder of Alibaba discusses in an innovative and insightful way how to hire and retain key employees. https://www.youtube.com/watch?v=brc_RfOmyHo

 **tips/ideas**

Tip: Be careful who you retain!

Employee retention strategies control the difference between valuable employees and those who do not bring much to the table. Therefore, for employee retention strategies to be implemented effectively, the organisation needs to recognise the value of the employee. A valuable employee is one who is loyal to the organisation, puts in the greatest effort and creates the desired results, contributing to the development of the organisation.

2. *Provide a well-defined career path*

    By mapping out a well-defined career path, employees have the ability to understand their prospects at the organisation.

Understanding one's options allows for security and stability. In this way, those who are able to pre-plan their career and are able to see the potential growth on offer at the organisation, are more likely to stay.

3.   *Offer a great total rewards package*

Remuneration is, for some people, one of the largest factors of employee retention. Employees always have high hopes and expectations when it comes to remuneration. It is, after all, their means of living. It also assigns perceived worth to an individual. An enticing remuneration package thus plays a very strong part in retention – especially when talent is in high demand and markets are tight.

An attractive reward package takes salaries, wages, bonuses, leave, shares, work-life balance, career, meaningful work and other such aspects, into account.

Remuneration components

- Salary and monthly wage - The largest component of the remuneration package, these allow for a comparison of employees, acting as a representation for the skills, abilities, knowledge and experience of an individual. Increases should be given per annum, based on an individual's performance as well as their contribution to the organisation.

- Bonus - Cash payments most commonly granted to employees at the end of the year.

- Benefits – These include paid and unpaid leave, holidays paid for by the company, health insurance, company car, etc.

- Long-term incentives (LTIs) - Share schemes.

- Retirement plans - These are payments an employee receives after they retire, such as provident funds.

- Other forms of remuneration - This includes services such as psychological counselling, gym membership, legal assistance, employee discounts and other such means of remuneration.

---

4. *Offer opportunities for advancement, training and growth*

People put work into their organisations and expect to receive remuneration and growth in return. An organisation should thus provide training, not only for employees' current roles but also for cross functional growth, so they can develop new skills and perform greater roles within the organisation. Their growth within the organisation tells them that they are able to exercise their worth and grow simultaneously.

5. *Offer work-life effectiveness*

With the world becoming more mobile, jobs are becoming increasingly flexible; there is less need for employees to be at the office, and with globalisation and people working on an international basis, organisations have different hours of functioning. Flexi-time is thus becoming increasingly common. This allows an employee to work in the hours they are most productive, from where they most desire, whilst allowing for leisure activities such as golf, gym or spending more time with one's family. Organisations that offer flexibility are those that have the highest retention rates.

See how Ricardo Semler, author of the *7 Day Weekend*, describes work-life effectiveness. His phenomenal company is worth reading about.

https://www.ted.com/talks/ricardo_semler_how_to_run_a_company_with_almost_no_rules#t-37496

6. *Afford job security*

In the current working world, downsizing, mergers, acquisitions and layoffs are increasingly common, reducing job security. Organisations that offer job security are thus those that thrive.

7. *Match the individual to the job*

    As individuals differ, so their preferences and abilities need to be
    matched to their jobs in order for them to have job satisfaction.
    A mismatch between knowledge, skills, abilities and jobs can
    lead to turnover. This is true for over or under qualification;
    those who are overqualified may feel bored, while those who
    are underqualified may feel they are not coping. Workload
    demands and job accomplishments that are unsatisfactory for
    the employee also lead to turnover. Burnout may result from
    work overload as well as geographic locations, and the ability of
    an individual to balance the work-life seesaw ultimately affects
    their retention. For these reasons, it is especially important to
    match the individual with their preferences and capabilities to
    ensure effective retention, and to offer tasks that can challenge
    key talent.

8. *Match expectations*

    Often, employee dissatisfaction occurs when there is a mismatch
    between expectations of work and reward. It is thus important
    for leadership to sit down with employees and clearly discuss
    and liaise with them regarding what is expected of them and
    what rewards they will receive in return. This allows them to
    understand exactly what they are receiving and not encounter
    any 'surprises'.

9. *Encourage positive work relationships by means of training and
    empathy*

    As the saying goes, "People don't quit jobs, they quit managers".

    Supervisory management as well as co-worker relations affect
    employee retention. An employee works directly with their
    manager and spends a lot of time taking instructions and
    performing their job accordingly. It is little wonder, then, that
    their satisfaction at the company is based on their relationship
    with their manager. It is important for managers to undergo

training so as to have empathetic skills as well as a positive, approachable attitude.

Additionally, by allowing flexibility, by providing support and feedback in a positive manner that recognises the efforts and performance of employees, and by supporting career planning development, employees feel they have a support system. This results in feelings of loyalty towards superiors and therefore the organisation. Good relationships with co-workers also lead to a positive atmosphere and increased retention rates.

10. *Provide timeous, consistent feedback*

Employees appreciate consistent feedback that is provided in a timeous manner. This allows them to understand when they are deviating from the path of the organisational objectives and correct themselves accordingly before they have wasted copious time and effort on a task. Consistent feedback in a timely manner is therefore seen as keeping employees in the loop, as well as being respectful towards the work they put in.

11. *Explain people's contributions to the objectives of the organisation*

Employees might not understand the value they are contributing to the organisation through their work tasks, and may thus feel frustrated at times. Explaining the reason they are performing a task and how they are contributing to the organisational objectives as a whole allows them to understand the value they are bringing to the organisation and understand their place in it, which contributes to retention.

12. *Provide a positive working environment*

When people feel like they belong at an organisation, Monday morning blues are rather upside down frowns. A work environment is considered conducive when the organisation has a strong organisational culture and good ethics.

13. *Provide a positive working culture*

It is important for an organisation to have a culture that resonates with employees and is underpinned by strong ethics. People tend to prefer organisational cultures that encourage learning, innovation and work-life balance. It is important for leadership to ensure that despite stressful deadlines, employees are provided with an enabling environment in which to manage their stress.

14. *Recognition*

Employees want to know that their efforts are worth something, which is why it is important to draw attention to their achievements and celebrate their successes.

15. *Be transparent and fair*

Reviews that are transparent and fair allow employees to gain a clearer picture of their performance. The review process should thus appraise the important milestones the employee has achieved, focusing on strengths and areas of development as well as ensuring a discussion on goal setting.

If all the above steps are taken into account, employee retention stands a better chance. In the end, employees are people and they want to feel that the effort they put in is acknowledged, as work plays a major aspect of everyday life.

The taxonomy of retention is set out nicely in the figure below. Ideally, one needs to align all of the boxes.

FACTORS THAT AFFECT EMPLOYEE RETENTION			
JOB	**CULTURE**	**PERSONAL**	**EXTERNAL**
Challenging, interesting, meaningful work	Management perceived as competent	Match with personal and family commitments	Economic climate – how readily other jobs are available
Meets expectations in terms of salary and conditions	Supportive leadership and management style	Geographic location	Competition from other industries
Offers training to upgrade skills in the workplace	Meets expectations in terms of co-workers	Confidence in own marketable skills and experience	Past employment experiences (good and bad)
Offers career development opportunities	Provides recognition and rewards for good work	Age (fit with workforce)	Community view of industry, business and job
Good work can be identified and recognised	Gives a sense of security about the company	Health (impacts on and from the job)	
Status of the position (more for management and senior roles)	Company values match with personal values		
Additional and long service leave and superannuation benefits			

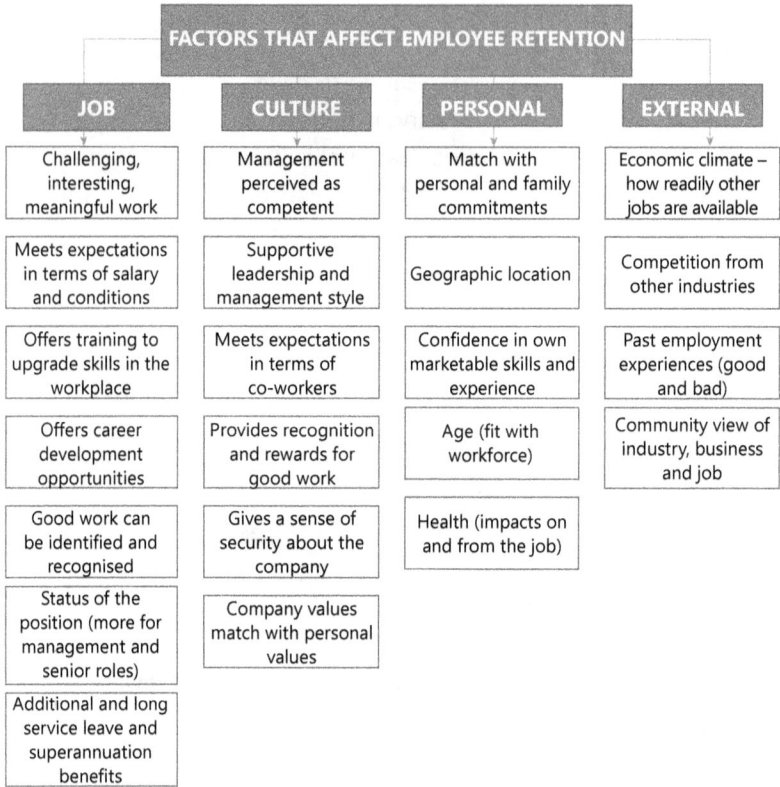

Figure 1: Factors that effect employee retention[6]

The debate will continue for another 100 years as to which of these factors is the most important. I have always held the view that top of the pile is inspirational leadership, followed closely by knowing how your job fits in to achieve the big picture. Many organisations turn to remuneration too quickly. I believe that it just has to be fair – that is the ticket to the game. Long may the debate live!

Employees who love what they do and where they work have a much stronger likelihood of remaining at the organisation. Retention strategies contribute to a preferential work environment and influence an employee's loyalty and commitment to the organisation. Teambuilding strategies and the like impact on employee engagement in a positive manner and amplifes employee morale.

Quick tip:

Let your employees have a longer lunch break, an extended weekend, a day where they can come in late. It lets them know the organisation cares about them and lets them get a breath of fresh air. You will see – it will even help their productivity.

What then, can be done to turn the tables on turnover?

Key retention interventions – guiding principles

Many initiatives may look good on paper, however some fundamental principles and guidelines are necessary to ensure the success of each. In Africa, many organisations are focussed on achieving these principles.

1.   **HR back to basics**

As a discipline, HR often suffers from a reputation gap between what they are trying to do and how they are perceived. Too often, HR teams are either too focussed on the administrative burden of transactional HR or too removed from the business, with high level strategic interventions that are not meeting the current need. Whilst both of these are necessary at different times, it is absolutely critical that the HR team is focused on getting the basics right, building their credibility, and becoming a trusted business partner. This requires the HR team to work and communicate as one united team that is focused on an HR strategy that is aligned to the business strategy. It also requires HR roles and measures to be unambiguous and realistic (with clearly defined roles of HR versus line). Every HR practitioner must understand the professional performance and competency standards and how they stack up, and regular engagement and consultation with line managers is key to ensure that priorities are being agreed upon and delivered. This requires specialist, business partner and administrative processes and people focused on the right activities.

Lastly, regular HR review sessions are needed to align activities, build capacity, build a sense of purpose and the team, and to hold each other accountable for performance. Ensure your HR team is effective and focussed before embarking on another new initiative, as it may run out of steam soon after the pilot if the team is not fully engaged and enabled to perform the roles required to make it work.

2. **Leadership brand**

Any change involving managers behaving differently toward staff has to be led by the leaders. Changing behaviour can be complex, but there are some golden rules. One of the first is to set the standard of what is expected of leaders. A leadership brand can do this. It defines an organisation's leadership philosophy, style and standards that are relevant not only to employees, but to all stakeholders. Typically a leadership brand consists of a handful of key statements of intent supported by measurable attributes.

It is important that the leadership brand is fully understood, bought into, and created with deep consultation throughout the organisation. Mechanisms need to be built into the fabric of the organisation that encourage, coach, and measure the leadership brand to ensure that key talent feel engaged and part of a great company with a great culture and great leaders.

3. **Values revitalisation**

    Whilst a communications campaign is often the first step
    in building an awareness of values, it is only the tip of the
    iceberg of what is required for a real values shift. Everyone
    joins an organisation with their own sets of values, beliefs and
    behaviours. It works better for everyone if alignment of these
    are checked during the recruitment phase and tested and
    encouraged during the induction phase. The real work, however,
    starts when a person joins teams, communicates with a certain
    style, builds relationships and makes decisions. This is where the
    leadership role is critical, and where counter-culture behaviour is
    identified, feedback given and coaching received to nip it in the
    bud. Where this behaviour is tolerated due to an avoidance of
    conflict or a lack of time and attention, the negative behaviour
    seems to be condoned and a culture of tolerance perpetuates,
    leading others to comment and criticise the culture.

    Values need to be on the radar of leaders at all times; they
    must be spoken about with passion, addressed with integrity
    and discussed in teams, and opportunities must be created for
    ongoing feedback and coaching. Often the leadership brand
    attributes will include an aspect of driving and role modelling
    the values to ensure that leaders are held accountable for their
    part.

    Values also need to be on the radar of employees at all times.
    Leaders should talk about them, hold team review sessions to
    identify how effectively the values are being demonstrated, and
    use visual aids to remind and encourage employees. It really
    helps if there is an opportunity to give feedback (upwards,
    sideways and downward) on the values through customised
    engagement surveys and a performance or competency review
    process.

4. **Building a coaching culture**

Coaching and mentoring have been proven to be among the most effective and cost-efficient means of achieving fast-tracked development, improved performance and a change in behaviours and attitudes. Given the widening gap in skills between experienced leaders, technical specialists, emerging managers and junior staff, passing on experience and skills through structured coaching has become a necessity. Coaching is one the fastest methods for building awareness and the practice required in high flyers for a step change in strategic thinking, problem solving, decision making, diversity management, resource management and finding collaborative approaches to difficult challenges. In addition, day-to-day management of the performance and development of talented individuals can best be done with a coaching style of leadership – looking for joint improvement goals and working on them together.

To be an effective coach (and manager) requires a targeted effort in learning and practicing the key skills of coaching, such as building rapport, listening, engaging, understanding how people learn and change, emotional intelligence, questioning, encouraging, confronting, development planning, etc. In organisations where this has been widely implemented, it has had a significant positive impact on the culture and the acquisition of new competencies.

Now that we have an idea of what retention is about, the next chapter will focus on the role that rewards play in the retention process.

Summary

Summary
- —
- —
- —

Summary of main points

■ Create meaningful work and show how the job fits in with the bigger vision of where the organisation is going.

■ Do not waste resources on retention measures for employees who are not contributing vastly to the organisation.

■ Retain talent that is difficult to find in a tight market.

■ Remuneration is not the only retention measure to be considered; retention comes as a package.

■ Show employees they are valued by making life easier for them. They will return the favour by means of loyalty and increased productivity.

Chapter 2

Retention of key talent and the role of rewards

This chapter covers:

- Key talent is important – why do they need special consideration in retention strategies?
- The role reward plays in retention.
- Types of retention strategies.
- A case study on retention.

Why retain key talent?

There are a number of reasons to retain key talent and put a special focus on these individuals – it makes good business sense:

- Retaining key talent (those employees who are the strongest performers, have high potential, or are in critical jobs) is particularly important during economic recoveries when organisations compete more aggressively for market share and talent.

- Key talent disproportionally contributes to current and future organisational performance, since key employees often become the organisation's leaders or employees with unique skills. In today's world you cannot hide your top talent because LinkedIn and other social media promote their capabilities and accomplishments.

- Furthermore, your top talent can compare the 'deal' or pay package they get from you with other organisations through websites such as salary.com, vault.com, glassdoor.com and onetonline.org.

The role of reward in retaining key talent

Over 600 reward professionals participated in a WorldatWork Association survey that focused on practices regarding key talent retention and the role of rewards. Since reward professionals are accountable for the design and execution of reward programmes and are often involved in assessing the causes of employee turnover, they have one of the best vantage points within the organisation as to how reward programmes impact the retention of key talent.

The study was designed to answer fundamental questions about key talent retention that included:

- Is retaining key talent a significant challenge?
- Are special efforts made to retain key employees?
- Why does key talent leave organisations?
- What is done to retain key talent and what is the effectiveness of these approaches?
- What role do counter-offers have in retaining key talent?
- Does organisational context determine how key talent retention efforts are managed?
- What are the best practices for retaining key talent?

Although the data is from 2012, it covers key projections to 2020 and the conclusions are just as valid today as they were then.

Trends in the retention of key talent

Estimates suggest that the cost of employee turnover often ranges from 50% to 200% of an employee's annual salary, based on the type and level of job they hold. These costs are substantial even for medium-sized organisations that have moderate rates of turnover (e.g. Allen[7] , Cascio[8] and O'Connell & Kung[9]). Losing key talent costs considerably more than typical employees, as their impact and contribution is greater and they are more difficult to replace.

Even though unemployment is still relatively high in many parts of the world, the U.S. and other industrial countries are already experiencing talent shortages in a number of labour markets. Employers report finding it difficult to fill engineering, high-skilled technical, managerial and executive, skilled trade and sales representative positions.[10] Finally, even when there are high unemployment rates, key talent is always in demand and an improving economy will exacerbate the challenge of retaining the most capable employees who have unique or critical skills.

WorldatWork predicts that not only is competition for key talent going to increase, but employee opinion norms indicate that 20% of employees plan to look for a new job in the next two years, and another 20% plan to leave their employers within the next five years.[11] These trends suggest discontent in the workforce, which is not surprising since employees are working harder as a result of turbulent economies and cost containment strategies. There have been limited base salary increases and incentive pay-outs awarded in recent years, and there has been increased pressure to perform. The trends may also highlight that the social contract surrounding the employment relationship is changing; because individuals and organisations have become more tenuously attached to each other, turnover has become a more prominent and accepted aspect of organisational life.

It is clear that one of the foremost challenges for management today is how to retain its key talent. Turnover is costly and directly impacts business performance, particularly during an economic recovery. As a result, reward professionals will be under increased pressure to make counter-offers, increase new hire offers, make more frequent exceptions to reward policies and programmes, and offer special deals and 'handcuff' mechanisms to retain key employees.

Is retaining key talent a significant challenge?

The survey[12] findings shown in Figure 2 point to the challenges organisations are facing in retaining key talent:

■ Most (81%) of the respondents recognised that turnover of key talent is very costly.

■ Over two-thirds (68%) of reward professionals said that employee retention is a major concern of senior management right now.

■ Over half (60%) expected turnover of key talent to increase substantially when the economy improves and said that the retention of key talent has become more difficult in recent months (58%).

■ Over half of the respondents were not confident in their organisation's ability to retain key talent as the economy improves (57%). In fact, 54% expected a substantial number of key employees to search for a better job as the economy improves.

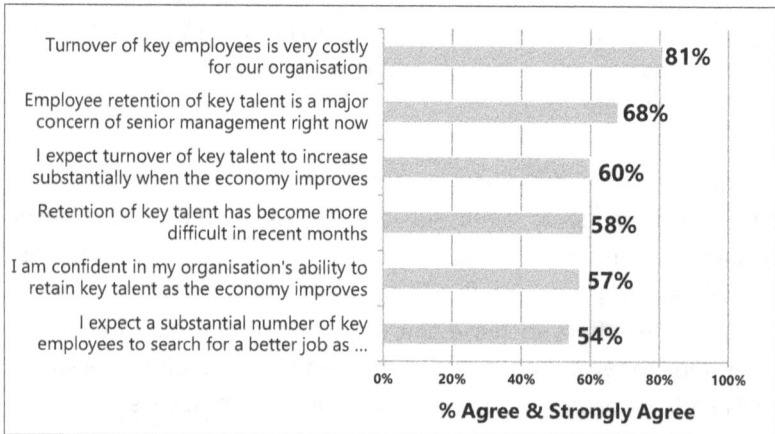

Figure 2: Is retaining employees a significant challenge?

(V) Self-check:

■ Have you calculated the direct and indirect costs of staff
turnover for your organisation?

■ Is retaining key talent considered one of your organisation's
top risks?

■ Are you confident you have the right retention strategies in
place to ensure that your talent is engaged and keen to stay?

Discussions with senior reward and HR professionals highlighted that
the retention of key talent is one of their top challenges, and they
worry about having the people necessary to win market share when
the economy improves. These professionals fear that key talent are
becoming increasingly frustrated in their organisations due to layoffs,
the resultant expansion of job accountabilities, and constraints on
reward programmes – primarily limited base salary increases, lower
incentives and fewer advancement opportunities.

These comments reinforce the message from survey respondents
that retention is a dominant organisational concern. Over 30% of
respondents reported turnover rates of key employees being over
10%, and 78% had turnover rates of over 5% for key employees.
When considering the cost of replacing these individuals, the price
is staggering. That leads us to the next question: "Are special efforts
made to retain key employees?"

Are special efforts made to retain key employees?

In order to make a special effort to retain key employees, you have to
know who they are. According to the findings shown in Figure 3:

■ over half (57%) of the organisations have a clear definition of key
talent and 66% have identified who those individuals are;

■ over 79% of respondents said that they define key talent to include employees who are top performers, have high potential, or are in critical jobs; and

■ while we know from other questions in the survey that 9% of respondents said that their organisations restrict their focus on key employees to top executives, the vast majority (75%) identify key talent below the executive level.

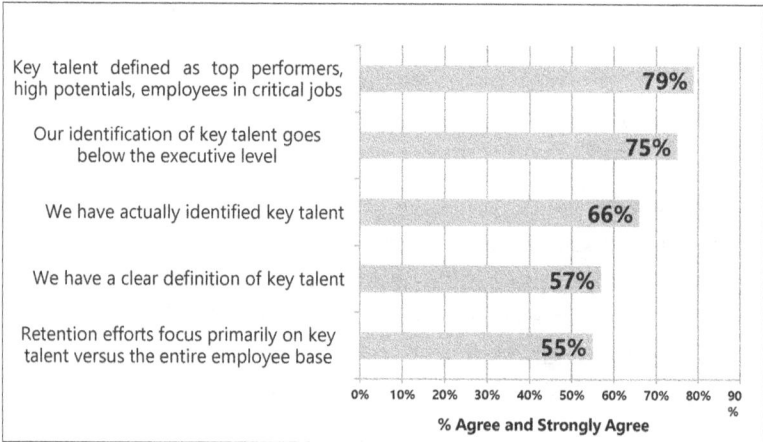

Figure 3: Identifying key talent

Self-check:

■ Has your organisation created a definition of key talent? Does it include the job, performance and level of expertise?

■ Has your organisation identified its key talent at all levels of the organisation?

The research showed that those people who said they were more confident in their ability to retain key talent during an economic recovery were more likely to report that their organisations are able to define key talent, have identified key talent, and have focused on key talent below the executive level. This shows that a best practice is to clarify the meaning of the term "key talent", define it to include a range of employee groups, and develop retention programmes targeted specifically for these groups.

Why does key talent leave organisations?

The general reasons for employees and talent leaving an organisation were outlined in Chapter 1. Figure 4 details the reasons why reward professionals believe that key talent leave their organisations. The percentages represent the respondents who agreed or strongly agreed for the stated reasons. The primary reasons given for quitting were:

- The opportunity to earn more pay elsewhere (77%). This contrasts sharply with the theory that money is not the main reason people leave. **There seems to be a big gap between theory and practice**!

- The next most cited reason is "lack of promotional opportunity" (67%).

- Feelings that pay levels are unfair relative to employees in other organisations (i.e. external equity) (58%)

- This was followed closely by "Dissatisfaction with job or work responsibilities" (58%).

- The fifth most identified reason for quitting was "pay levels perceived as unfair vs. employee performance" (53%).

One should note that three of the five frequently given reasons for quitting are directly tied to pay. In fact, the number two item, lack of promotional opportunities, could also be partially related to a desire for more remuneration.

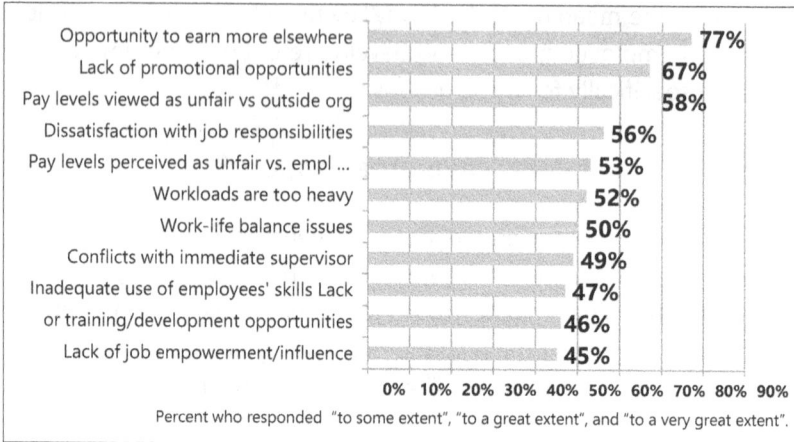

Figure 4: Most likely reasons why key talent quits

✅ Self-check:

■ Have you made an effort to better understand why people leave your organisation? Do you conduct exit interviews for all employees who leave? What other data points do you have to help explain turnover?

■ Do you know why people choose to stay in your organisation? Have you conducted any stay interviews with key talent?

■ Do you include the discussion of retention factors as a standard component of performance appraisals?

According to respondents, the least likely reasons for key talent to quit are for an opportunity for a better healthcare package (14%) or better retirement/saving benefit package (16%). Likewise, even during a significant downturn in the economy, reward professionals indicate that job security for key talent remains high.

Over two-thirds (71%) of respondents thought that fear of job loss and job insecurity were *either not an issue or an issue only to a minor extent* in turnover decisions. Both "easier commute" and "non-job related factors" also scored low as reasons why a key employee might quit (32% and 27% respectively).

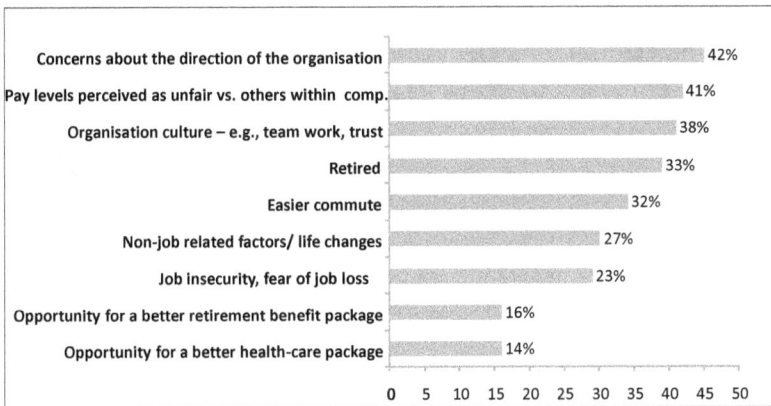

Figure 5: Least likely reasons why key talent quits

Knowing which factors may lead key talent to quit and which do not provides important insights for crafting methods to retain them.

What is done to retain key talent and what is the effectiveness of these approaches?

Figures 6 and 7 focus on the types of programmes organisations use to retain key talent and the perceived effectiveness of these efforts.

- Consistent with the responses to other questions, key talent identification is a core attribute in programmes that are deemed as effective in the retention of key employees (85%).

- Three-quarters of the respondents indicated that this strategy is either "effective" or "most effective".

- The other methods reportedly most often used to retain key employees include, "discussed their future with the organisation" (80%), "paid key employees above the labour market" (75%), "created a succession plan to replace individuals critical to success" (74%), "developed employees who may replace key employees who may leave" (73%), and "provided tuition reimbursement and other educational opportunities" (83%).

- Although "allowed for flexible hours or telecommuting" is down toward the bottom in terms of percent used (68%), it is toward the top of list in terms of evaluated effectiveness (67%).

- All of these programmes were perceived to be "effective" or "very effective" in the majority of cases (over 50% of the time).

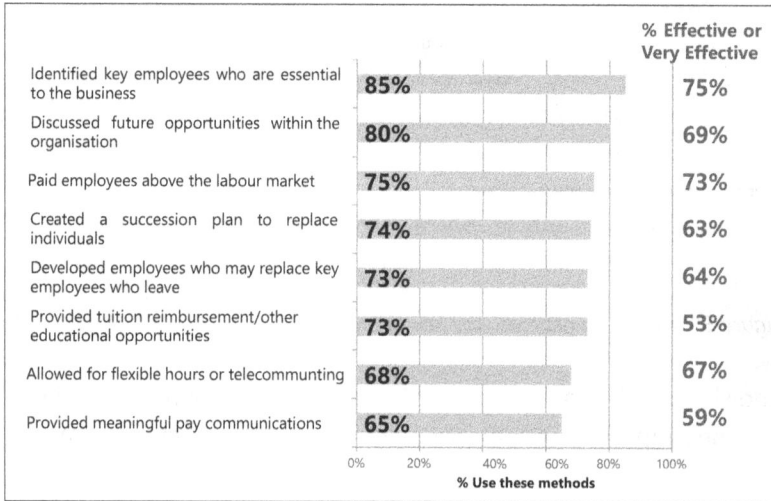

	% Use these methods	% Effective or Very Effective
Identified key employees who are essential to the business	85%	75%
Discussed future opportunities within the organisation	80%	69%
Paid employees above the labour market	75%	73%
Created a succession plan to replace individuals	74%	63%
Developed employees who may replace key employees who leave	73%	64%
Provided tuition reimbursement/other educational opportunities	73%	53%
Allowed for flexible hours or telecommuting	68%	67%
Provided meaningful pay communications	65%	59%

Figure 6: Methods most often used to retain key talent

Although over half of the respondents indicated that they use each of the methods listed in the survey as a means to enhance key talent retention, those that were *least likely to be used* were "provided mentors for key employees" (52%), "provided increased incentive or bonus opportunity to key employees" (54%), and "provided key employees with stock options or equity awards" (56%).

The methods deemed to be *the least effective* in retaining key talent were "provided tuition reimbursement and other educational opportunities" (53%), "provided mentors for key employees," and "provided meaningful pay communications, including total remuneration statements" (59%). One can note that the most frequently used methods are not necessarily the methods considered the most effective.

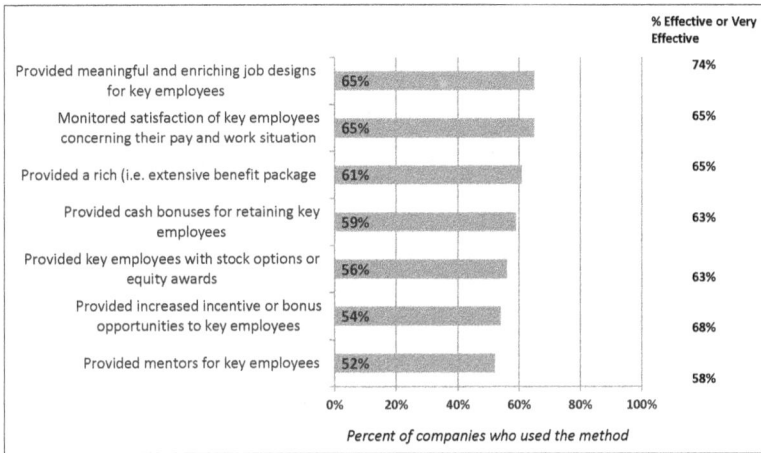

Figure 7: Least used methods to retain key talent

✓ Self-check:

■ What are the main retention strategies used in your organisation?

■ Which of these retention strategies are most effective and why?

■ Which of these retention strategies are least effective and why?

■ Are your indications of effectiveness based on your perceptions or those of your employees? Consider including the voice of the employee to make an informed assessment.

Checklist of strategies to retain key talent – in order of priority:

Strategy	✓ if used
Identify key talent	
Discuss with key talent their future with the organisation	
Pay above market level	
Create a succession plan for people critical to organisational success	
Develop employees who may replace the key talent	
Provide tuition reimbursements and other educational opportunities	
Allow for flexi hours or telecommuting	
Provide meaningful pay communications	
Provide meaningful job designs	
Monitor satisfaction with pay and work situation	
Provide a rich benefits package	
Provide cash bonuses	
Provide share options	
Provide mentors	

To determine if there were methods for retaining key talent that were overlooked, reward professionals were asked to respond to an open-ended question: "In terms of retention of key talent, what is your organisation doing that works particularly well?" They found that cash remuneration was most often identified as being the best method for retaining key employees.

Reward professionals definitely have opinions as to the effectiveness of different methods for the retention of key talent, but do they formally evaluate the effectiveness of these methods? The answer is mixed: 21% said they do not evaluate their key talent retention programmes and 31% said they rely only on informal feedback from employees and managers. However, 26% examine formal attitude surveys, 31% examine turnover data, and 7% conduct a return-on-investment (ROI) analysis on the subject.

What role do counter-offers play in retaining key employees?

Consistent with earlier counter-offer studies[13] , few organisations have a formal policy on counter-offers.

- 83% said that "We do not have a counter-offer policy; each situation is decided on a case-by-case basis".

- 14% said that they have "an informal policy (or practice) that provides general guidance". Only 4% said they have a formal written policy.

- For those organisations that have either a formal or informal policy, counter-offers are typically provided "only for key employees" (10%) or "at the request of the employee's supervisor or manager" (34%).

- Respondents said that extending a counter-offer either "seldom creates a problem" or "has created some problems", at 33% and 25% respectively.

- The majority of respondents indicated that the HR/remuneration function and management are either jointly involved in extending counter-offers (57%) or the "HR/Remuneration function may provide some input, but management primarily determines who receives a counter-offer and the nature of that counter-offer" (26%).

Does organisational context determine how key talent retention efforts are managed?

One question that is commonly asked is how context influences the degree to which key talent retention is considered a problem or what methods are more effective in retaining key employees. WorldatWork[14] found that organisation size, industry and sector has little impact on why high talent employees quit or the methods used to retain them. The only systematic impact was found across economic sectors. The private sector respondents (i.e. both privately held and publicly traded organisations) were more likely to identify and provide a definition of key talent than respondents in the public sector or non-profit sector. The public sector respondents were also less confident that they could retain key employees during an economic recovery than respondents from other sectors.

Retention in action – Findings from research in a development finance institution

CASE STUDY

Retention of high potential employees in a development finance company

Interviews were conducted with high potential employees in order to understand which factors could be used to retain such employees within the company. The study aimed to identify factors that could positively impact the retention of high potential employees in a development finance company.

The results of these interviews revealed the following themes:

Leadership and organisational culture

Participants valued the good leadership they experienced in the company. This was the leading retention factor expressed. Leaders who are accessible and inclusive inspire and motivate high potential employees within organisations.[15] Many of the participants cited leadership as the reason why they chose to leave their previous organisations and why they remained with their current employer. Participants appeared to respect their current leaders, particularly the CEO, who was described as a people's person who lives the culture he has created. This finding supports the view that leaders reflect culture.[16] Participants trusted leadership as a result of the good business ethics and personal integrity they observed.[17] Such identification appeared to influence retention positively. Participants stressed the importance of having leaders who motivate them, allow them the freedom to make decisions and enable them to work independently, but who are available and approachable if assistance is required. Such a leadership approach allows employees to take ownership of their actions, with the result that they remain engaged and committed to the company.[18]

The physical and cultural environment created by the company was a prominent theme in almost every interview. Participants agreed that the organisational culture encourages an environment that promotes innovation and collaboration.[19] The physical environment was also seen as a differentiating factor and one that fosters collaboration and innovation among employees, departments and customers. From the findings one can see that high potential employees prefer to work in environments that are productive, respect employees, value diversity, and are inclusive and sociable.[20]

Organisational purpose

Participants made reference to the importance of belonging to an organisation that has a motivational purpose to which they are able to relate. Participants mentioned that, as they live and work in a developing country, it is important for them, at this stage of their careers as senior managers or specialists, to see the value in what they do. They want to belong to an organisation that is committed to improving the country and one that focuses on sustainability. Many of the participants enjoyed the direct impact that the organisation has on communities and the economy and, for them, this was a powerful motivator, increasing their desire to stay at the company. The findings confirmed that if high potential employees identify with the organisation's purpose and recognise their role in fulfilling that purpose, they are likely to remain with the organisation.[21]

Developmental opportunities

The need to develop was evident among these high potential participants. All expressed appreciation for the developmental opportunities provided, which they considered to be abundant in assisting them to grow, achieve and advance in their careers. Similarly, Ryan[22] found that it is important for high potential employees to work for a company that provides them with such opportunities. Although developmental opportunities did not appear to be the leading retention factor for the participants, it emerged within the top three factors.

Many of the participants felt that the organisation offered a variety of developmental opportunities which were tailored and customised to their differing needs. They appreciated that the organisation supported continuous learning and development. Allen[23] and Mohlala, Goldman and Goosen[24] confirmed that high potential employees appreciate organisational investment in training and skills development, with Allen[25] noting that providing training and developmental opportunities generally increases the retention of high potential employees.

Meaningful work

A common theme that emerged was the meaningfulness of the work which the company provides. Participants felt that their jobs add value and that they are able to see the value of their roles in the company's success.

Their jobs allow them to be integrally involved in the business and they are able to make strategic business decisions. Participants alluded to the fact that if they were no longer challenged or if they could not see the value of their work, they would leave the company.[26]

Participants expressed a similar view to that of Ramlall,[27] stating that at this stage of their careers they were on a constant journey to become better versions of themselves in the work place. They needed to add value and fulfil their personal passion; their roles are meaningful to them personally and this motivates them. Participants explained that the meaningfulness of their work drives their commitment to the organisation and due to their involvement in the business they do not wish to seek other employment.

Collegiality

Participants explained how they value and respect the people who work for the organisation. They enjoy coming to work because of the people with whom they work and interact, and they respect the teams in the business and those who they referred to as their organisational heroes. High potential employees need to work in an organisation where they feel respected and, more importantly, where they respect the people they work with.[28]

Relationships appear to be a factor that influences the retention of high potential employees, as the participants enjoyed being surrounded by people who are hardworking and passionate. Employees enjoy working with people who are like-minded and share the same behavioural norms.[29] Participants were complimentary about both teams and individuals employed within the company. There was a clear level of respect and appreciation for different people, teams and qualities within the business, reflective of the culture created to which high potential employees relate. This finding is aligned to the prior research of Paul and Berry[30] and Ramlall.[31]

Conclusion

There is increasing focus on retaining high potential employees.[32] Organisational leaders and HR practitioners are also concerned about the costs and the time it takes to replace high performers.[33] The 2012 WorldatWork Research Survey[34] indicated that key talent are very concerned with their reward packages, thus to retain them the reward system must be perceived as relevant, differentiated and fair. Furthermore, management should consider paying differential pay treatments across most reward elements to lessen the chances that competitors can lure them away. Careful monitoring of the external labour market for key talent is advisable, but one must also make sure that employees identified as top talent understand why they are paid what they are paid. A reward system designed to differentiate key talent from other employees is important to enhance perceptions that the pay system is fair.

Key talent are also concerned about their opportunity for development and advancement, thus management should have development and succession planning processes in place for each key employee. Furthermore, key employees should be kept apprised of their development and advancement opportunities. Although it may be tempting to leave a key employee in a position, this can create retention problems when their advancement is perceived as being slow. Management should monitor voluntary turnover among key employees and make sure that they understand why they leave so more effective strategies for retaining key employees can be developed. Retaining key talent is challenging and numerous factors indicate that key talent is going to become even scarcer in the future. To survive in a competitive global economy, management must develop strategies for attracting, developing and retaining key talent. This requires a carefully developed HR strategy and the coordinated efforts of senior management, HR and reward professionals to effectively manage this challenge.

Now that the link between retention and rewards has been discussed, the next chapter will focus on the relationship between retention and engagement.

Summary of main points

- Over 50% of reward professionals believe that key talent retention will be challenging in the future.
- Organisations that identify, define and manage key talent deeper into the organisation are more confident that they will be able to retain these individuals.
- Key talent leave organisations for a variety of reasons, with perceived inadequate rewards being the main reason.
- A certain method of retaining key talent may be effective for one organisation but ineffective for another.

Chapter 3

Retention and engagement

....

This chapter covers:

- ▣ What drives retention?

- ▣ What is engagement, and what role does it play in retention?

- ▣ What are "hot skills", "scarce skills", and "critical skills", and how do we retain them?

- ▣ What is the business case for engagement?

According to global research conducted by the Corporate Leadership Council Advisory Board, about 25% of the "stay" decision relates to remuneration.[35] This is a critical 25%, but it is just a ticket to the game. Reward drives attraction and retention in the short term, but regardless of reward, employees still leave companies for many other reasons. Most commonly, employees leave because of dissatisfaction with their managers and leaders. When looking at retention strategies, the best option is to spend resources on developing managers and on leadership skills. Only then should reward packages be considered. There are many options in developing reward strategies. This chapter discusses the remuneration trends that relate to retention.

....

Engagement
....

Organisations often implement attraction and retention strategies and schemes. Some work, but many do not. The unintended consequence is that employers may be fuelling the frenzy and driving pay costs higher. Perhaps the time has come to implement robust employee engagement strategies. After all, there is a high correlation between engaged employees and the bottom line.

One of the characteristics of the knowledge economy is the high level of mobility of knowledge workers. This cost, in both financial and non-financial terms, is high. Staff turnover is expensive and finding replacement skills can be a difficult task. The era of the knowledge worker is here, and with an individual skills base, workers have the intellectual clout to move themselves to whatever attractive offer may arise. The main challenge this leaves for the employer is how to retain key talent when the demand for skills is so much greater than the supply.

The definition of "retain" has two meanings: "to hold or keep in possession" and "to engage the services of". The traditional focus in many HR practices has been to hold or keep rather than to engage a service. High-value employees and those with "hot" skills want to be "engaged" and not "kept". Organisations need to shift their thinking and focus on what they need to do to help these employees become fully engaged in the organisation. Perhaps the focus should be to engage people for as long as possible, rather than trying to retain them for as long as possible. An innovative retention strategy and an organisation reward strategy would certainly aid this process.

Part of engaging knowledge workers means providing an environment where skills transferral and knowledge-sharing are easily facilitated. After an organisation brings new employees in through the door and has filled all of its hot-skills positions, it cannot rest. The reality is that someone is going to leave relatively soon. What should be done is to transfer that knowledge immediately – almost the second that new employees walk through the door.

Conceptualisation of employee engagement

Research has shown that engagement is not something that happens overnight; it is something that needs to be built into the corporate culture. It is a matter of keeping one's ear to the ground, understanding and monitoring engagement, and dealing with issues as quickly as they emerge, including instantaneous recognition of top employees. What engages employees is the feeling that they are making a difference in the work that they care about, that they are working with people who share their mission and values, and that their organisation respects them as adults.

Engagement can make a huge difference to performance. **Improving employee engagement is not exceptionally difficult or expensive**. A lot of the drivers of engagement are subtle issues and do not require a large amount of capital outlay.

See the following Ted Talk to further understand employee engagement: https://www.ted.com/talks/ dan_ariely_what_makes_us_feel_good_about_ our_work

A comparison across countries - drivers of engagement, attraction and retention

Towers Perrin carried out two sets of research, one in the United States and one across six countries in Europe. They asked both groups questions on a variety of workplace factors in their organisation – practices, processes, culture, leadership style, and development opportunities. In other words, they probed all the key elements typically seen to be the drivers of workforce behaviour.

In Chapter 1, a general outline of retention drivers was outlined. Towers Perrin directed their studies to the "top 10" drivers of attraction, retention and engagement in Europe and the United States. While there were some similarities between the European and the US reports, the key factors were quite widely divergent in each list. The results of the comparative studies are shown in the following tables.

Table 2: Top 10 drivers of attraction, engagement and retention in Europe

	Top 10 attraction drivers	Top 10 engagement drivers	Top 10 retention drivers
1	Work-life balance	Senior management interest in employees	Manager inspires enthusiasm for work
2	Recognition for work	Ability to improve skills	Career advancement opportunities
3	Career advancement opportunities	Senior management to demonstrate values	Company reputation as a good employer
4	Challenging work	Challenging work	Fair and consistent pay determination
5	Competitive pay	Decision-making authority	Intention of working after retirement in another field
6	Learning/ development opportunities	Company reputation as a good employer	Decision-making authority
7	Job autonomy	Ability to influence company decisions	Overall work environment
8	Variety of work	Company focus on customer satisfaction	Intention of working after retirement to stay active
9	Pay rises linked to individual performance	Fair and consistent pay determination	Manager provides access to learning opportunities
10	Company reputation as a good employer	Overall work environment	Senior management demonstrates values

Table 3: Top 10 drivers of attraction, engagement and retention in the United States of America

	Top 10 attraction drivers	Top 10 engagement drivers	Top 10 retention drivers
1	Competitive healthcare benefits	Senior management interest in employees	Career advancement opportunities
2	Competitive pay	Challenging work	Retention of high-calibre people
3	Work-life balance	Decision-making authority	Overall work environment
4	Competitive retirement benefits	Company focus on customer satisfaction	Ability to improve skills
5	Career advancement opportunities	Career advancement opportunities	Resources to get job done
6	Challenging work	Company reputation as a good employer	Competitive pay
7	Calibre of co-workers	Collaboration with co-workers	Clear goals from manager
8	Pay rises linked to individual performance	Resources to get job done	Challenging work
9	Recognition for work	Ability to influence company decisions	Manager inspires enthusiasm for work
10	Company reputation as a good employer	Senior management vision	Overall satisfaction with benefits

There are some common threads that should not be ignored. It is believed that these results are transferrable and are universal truths.

Checklist – Rate each item from 1 to 10 on how you believe your organisation would rate

Driver	Attraction	Engagement	Retention
Competitive healthcare benefits			
Competitive pay			
Work-life balance			
Competitive retirement benefits			
Career advancement opportunities			
Challenging work			
Calibre of co-workers			
Pay rises linked to individual performance			
Recognition for work			
Company reputation as a good employer			

Key talent skills

"Hot skills"

A shortage of staff with "hot skills" is unlikely to be quickly alleviated. An organisation's success may increasingly depend on these workers and its ability to attract and retain key talent critical to organisational competency.

 Self-check:

The following questions could serve as a template:

- What are the hot skills critical to your organisation?
- Who possesses those skills?
- What is important to the people who have these skills?
- What is needed to develop and transfer these skills continuously?

Hot skills categories

Cognisance should be taken of these prevailing categories and skill levels. Attraction and retention options are suggested for each category.

Critical skills

These are the skills categorised as essential for the sustainability and effective service delivery of an organisation's mandates, and are based on core business requirements. Should the employees holding down these skilled positions leave the organisation, it would be significantly affected because of the considerable impact on the operations of the organisation should the position remain vacant for any period of time.

Scarce skills

These skills are based on market supply and demand factors. In many instances, scarce skills are also critical to the organisation and may receive the same remuneration treatment for both categories. This is particularly apparent in highly technically advanced areas. It is therefore important to determine whether the scarce skills as determined by the market are also critical enough within the organisation to warrant special remuneration treatment.

These skills reflect the supply and demand of a particular skill at a particular time. The skill requirement may not necessarily mean it is complex, but could imply that, owing to circumstances, only a few people in the market have these specific skills. The situation changes over time when skill pipelining or the completion of large projects facilitates more people acquiring this level of skills, negating their "hot skills" status:

- Base pay - In order not to distort the salary scales within an organisation, these employees would be paid within the applicable grade range. It should be ensured that the guaranteed portion is in line with the appropriate levels of employees within the same grade.

- Variable pay - This part of the employee's total remuneration includes variable pay components such as a performance incentive scheme or a reward and recognition scheme. Measurable targets should be in place, and the pay-outs of these schemes should be in line with the rest of the organisation's remuneration policy.

- Market premiums and allowances - A scarce skills premium may be placed over and above the salary. By keeping the salary constant, the incumbent can be brought back to the appropriate base pay should supply and demand factors change. The scarce skills premium is a market premium over and above the base pay. The premium will be on top of guaranteed pay as a "bonus premium" and can be removed once the supply and demand situation has changed. Market premiums are not guaranteed, and the quantum should be in line with the market rate to complement a guaranteed basic pay. These premiums are not regarded as part of the employee's guaranteed portion of pay, but should be taken into account when comparisons are done on total cost to company per employee. It is important to note that not all scarce skills are equal, therefore suggesting a standard market premium would be the wrong approach. Each position should be interrogated and the size of the premium determined by the gap in the market. The premium is usually expressed as a percentage of the midpoint of the organisation's pay scale, and the same level of premium is paid to individuals irrespective of their position within that scale (to be illustrated further down).

High fliers

These skills reflect a very high level of consistent competence and performance over a long period of time and tend to attract the attention of an organisation's executive management.

Employees in this category consistently display an improvement in performance and skills level over a long period. They may be innovative, have wisdom, and command authority over their areas of influence by virtue of their wisdom, and so on. They also command respect among their peers in the field. Their market value increases over time and they will command relatively higher pay.

- Basic salary - Pay should be gradually moved towards the market upper quartile. Pay scales will adjust according to the market and consequently, employees can be maintained at the upper quartile level or higher, depending on the consistency and level of superior performance.

- Variable pay - These employees would generally earn larger performance incentives than their peers based on the attainment of robust performance measures.

- Market premiums and allowances - Once these employees are paid at the upper quartile, a premium above this level may be considered to retain their services. This is, however, not common practice, and any variable pay is usually catered for in the bonus scheme where the employee, because he or she is a top performer, usually achieves the stretch targets and resultant relatively high level of bonus.

Critical skills

Since this category of skills is critical for organisations to sustain their business objectives, the most appropriate strategy must be sought and applied to suit specific objectives. These interventions will ensure that the organisation is able to retain the skills that are essential for business continuity.

Attraction and retention options include:

- Higher basic salary: To stay competitive, payment for critically-skilled employees will usually focus on the 75th market percentile (upper quartile). This will enable managers of these staff members to ensure that the guaranteed portion of their packages is competitive, both to attract and motivate skills identified as critical. To this end, it is crucial that the organisation subscribes to a robust remuneration survey so that accurate market quartiles can be determined.

- Variable pay: This part of the employee's total remuneration includes variable pay components such as a performance incentive scheme or a reward and recognition scheme. Measurable targets should be in place, and the pay-outs of these schemes should be targeted at a competitive market quartile.

- Market premiums and allowances: As per the base pay description above, critical skills are usually catered for within the organisation's pay scales and do not attract premiums or allowances based on external market comparisons. There are, however, cases where job family-specific pay scales are created to reflect the market should the current scales (by grade) not sufficiently cater for these skills. This method is, however, often an administrative burden and is driven by scarcity in the market. In these cases, both the critical skills and scarce skill remuneration treatments are applied to the position, thereby not increasing the organisation's fixed costs. This is illustrated in the figure below.

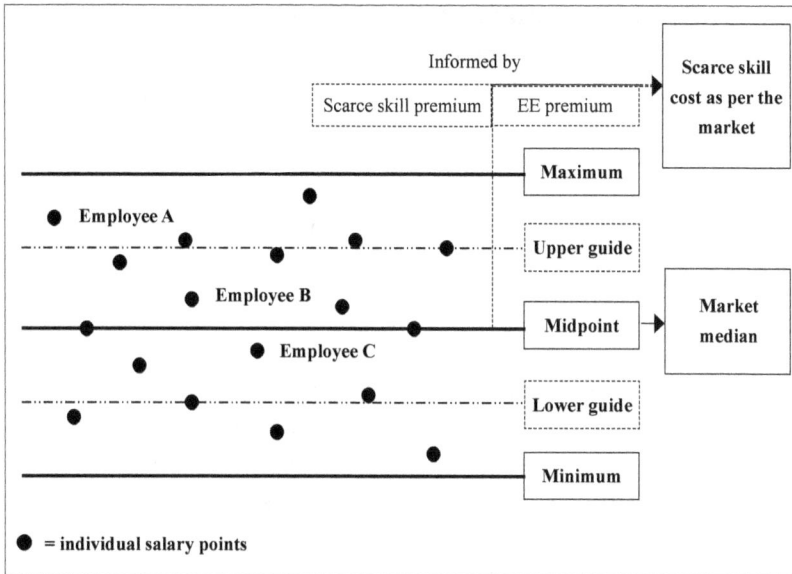

Figure 8: Hot skills remuneration treatment

Pay scale design

In the example shown in the figure above, the organisation's pay scales have been aligned to the market median, and the midpoint of the above scale has been anchored at this market quartile. A spread has then been applied to either side of this midpoint to create the minimum and maximum salary levels for the scale. This would be done for every grade level within the organisation and employees paid within this range.

Remuneration options

Employee A could be a critical skill or a high-flier. This is evident by the employee's position in the pay scale in relation to his or her peers. Because Employee A is paid above the upper guide of the pay scale, he or she is effectively being paid at a higher market point than Employee C. As salary scales move in line with the market, the only way that an employee should be able to get to that point would be through consistently good performance. The employee would move through the scales more quickly than his or her peers (high-fliers) as a result of higher increases or if their skill was deemed critical, and paid around the upper guide or maximum of the pay scale to reflect a different market quartile (the upper quartile, if the pay scale is wide enough).

Let us assume that both Employee B and Employee C have scarce skills. Their scarce skill premium would be determined by the cost of that scarce skill in the market, or an agreed premium would be applied.

In the first scenario, the difference between the midpoint of the salary scale and the "market cost" of the scarce skill is what would determine the level of premium payable. This premium would then apply to both Employee B and Employee C, even though their salary levels are different. In other words, it applies to the skill category and not the employee. The same would hold true for employment equity employees, as per the example above.

Another approach that is often used is to apply an agreed premium to certain levels of skill. An example of how this could work can be seen in the table below. Let us assume that in an organisation, all skill categories are not equal, i.e. it is possible to pay different premiums for the technical, engineering and IT skills categories.

Table 4: An approach to premiums for skills shortages

Description	Percentage premium
Most extreme shortage of skills. At least 25% or more of these posts have been vacant in the past year. Offers have been made, but the pay scales alone cannot attract the required skills to join the organisation due to scarcity premiums or evidence exists of high turnover in the order of 25% or more.	10% of the applicable pay scale midpoint

Description	Percentage premium
Extreme shortage of skills. At least 10 to 25% of these posts have been vacant in the past year. Offers have been made, but the pay scales alone cannot attract the required skills to join the organisation due to scarcity premiums or evidence exists of high turnover in the order of 10 to 25%.	7.5% of the applicable pay scale midpoint
Shortage of skills. At least 5 to 10% of these posts have been vacant in the past year. Offers have been made, but the pay scales alone cannot attract the required skills to join the organisation due to scarcity premiums or evidence exists of high turnover in the order of 5 to 10%.	5% of the applicable pay scale midpoint

Business case for investing in employee engagement

It is critical for the organisation to spell out its reasons for following the route of employee engagement. The business case for employee engagement becomes an imperative benefit in order to increase the proportion of engaged employees. The importance of engagement to employee retention and total shareholder return, as well as organisational branding, cannot be under estimated.

According to Towers Perrin, research shows that companies with higher levels of employee engagement outperform their competitors in terms of profitability. Managers must first understand what engages their employees and what factors drive engagement in their companies. Employees will be happier and more productive, which ultimately leads to a positive impact on business results.

Employee engagement also acts as a catalyst towards the retention of staff and is critical to any organisation that seeks not only to retain valued employees, but also to increase its levels of performance. One of the most important drivers of an employee's intention to leave is his or her level of commitment to the organisation.

Work/home life effectiveness

Business has recognised that employees live in a society and the balance between work and home life is important in order to obtain a more engaged workforce. A lack of interest or neglect by corporate management in this area leads to high cases of burnout caused by increasing stress, with a resultant drop in productivity.

Research recently coined "burnout" to describe the erosion of work engagement. Data from the Gallup Employee Engagement Index offers insight into the degree to which engagement levels at work may affect employees' attitudes and behaviour away from the office.

Quick tip:

In a world where it is now possible, flexi-time offers the most appropriate means of work-life balance.

CASE STUDY

The cost of disengagement in the United States and the United Kingdom

The Gallup Organisation's employee engagement survey, using the results of its engagement index and national average for productivity and salary as a base, estimates that actively disengaged employees cost American businesses between $270 and $343 billion a year. This includes high rates of absenteeism and staff turnover from this sector of employees.

In the United Kingdom, using similar census data on the number of working adults, their average salary and productivity, Gallup estimated that the productivity gap among actively disengaged employees costs somewhere between £43 and £44 billion a year.

Gallup used responses to seven core statements as the parameters for defining "engagement":

- I understand how my work contributes to the organisation's overall success.

- I am personally motivated to help the organisation succeed.

- I am willing to put in a great deal of effort beyond what is normally expected.

- I have a sense of personal accomplishment from my job.

- I would recommend the organisation to a friend as a good place to work.

- The organisation inspires me to do my best work.

- The organisation's values are aligned with my personal values.

Quick tip:

These are fundamental questions to assess the extent of your employees' engagement. This should be done at least once every three years, together with "stay" interviews, i.e. asking what makes your employees stay in the organisation. Use the statement in the above case study to develop the survey.

The link between engagement and financial performance

In the US study, Towers Perrin moved this data one step further. They collected financial data for respondents' companies (where they were publicly listed – a sample of approximately 5,000 companies) and began to calculate links between those respondents' scores on certain engagement factors with their companies' overall financial performance.

It is interesting to note that the analysis showed a direct correlation between employee engagement itself and revenue growth.
The implications of the study are quite apparent. The power of discretionary effort by highly-engaged employees on multiple levels can be seen, for example, in the service business, where an engaged employee has been proven to focus on customer service and excellence, and in doing so improves customer loyalty and retention. Business indirectly benefits as revenue grows and behaviour modelling and performance culture improve.

The effect of engagement on total shareholder return

Hewitt also conducted a different financial analysis of its full database of 2,000 'Best Employer' companies in over 50 countries worldwide, including client and former client companies and those that had taken part in Hewitt's 'Best Employer' listings, to measure the correlation between high engagement levels among employees and total shareholder return (TSR) to the organisations.

Tracking the results of Hewitt's engagement surveys over a period of four years with the TSR of those companies, a positive correlation was found between the two. In short, companies that had between 60% to 100% of employees engaged (in Hewitt's classification system, where the average organisation has 49% of employees engaged) showed an impressive average TSR of 20.2% for the period. In comparison, those companies with moderate levels of engagement (49% to 60% engaged employees) had an average TSR of 5.6%, and companies with fewer than 40% engaged employees had a negative TSR (–9.6%).

Although this is a straight correlation, Hewitt contends that their individual client work shows that engagement has a causal relationship with business performance and not vice versa. This conclusion is based on the number of companies they have seen improve their results after specifically focusing on engagement.

One of the most practical models of engagement, the Five Pillars of Engagement, was developed by Accenture. The five pillars are shown in Figure 9 below.

1 RECOGNISE AND REWARD SUPERIOR PERFORMANCE	**2** ESTABLISH A LEARNING ENVIRONMENT	**3** CREATE KNOWLEDGE-SHARING COMMUNITIES	**4** MANAGE THE CULTURE OF CHANGE	**5** PROVIDE OPPORTUNITIES TO GROW AND DEVELOP
Organisations can foster a culture of belonging by rewarding and recognising employees based on both individual and business performance. Individual performance should be judged not only on financial contributions (such as meeting sales targets), but on other contributions as well, such as superior customer service or innovative process improvements. Make sure rewards are not only financial; consistent recognition for a job well done through frequent informal praise, organisation award programmes, perks, parties or other means will go far towards establishing a culture that values individuals' contributions.	Organisations with the most engaged workforces provide a significant number of learning opportunities for employees to excel. To establish a learning culture, offer plenty of formal learning opportunities (such as classroom or online courses), but also provide lots of informal learning experiences (eg mentoring programmes, "lunch and learns", observational feedback or specific assignments designed to sketch a person's capabilities). Additionally, provide employees with managers who are capable and willing to review an employee's learning needs frequently, to ensure that they align with career plans and goals.	Engaged employees feel supported by a culture in which knowledge, information and resources are easily shared. Many organisations try to achieve this culture by providing web-based tools that enable employees to access knowledge capital. However, knowledge databases can become unwieldy and littered with excessive, irrelevant information. Organisations can address this problem by providing information based on employees' roles in the organisation or by providing training on effective use of such tools. In addition, encourage other forms of knowledge sharing, such as communities of practice that enable employees to share insights and experience.	Workforces committed to an organisation's goals must understand both what the goals are and how they are being affected or executed through changes such as mergers, acquisitions, or the outsourcing of key business processes. Communicating details about major organisational changes in a timely fashion will foster a culture of trust and belonging, and help employees pursue organisational goals more effectively. Programmes designed to reduce any negative impact of such changes on morale and productivity (such as assigning "buddies" to newly acquired employees) will also ensure that engagement levels remain high.	Few employees feel committed if they are not given opportunities for career development. Our research suggests that to foster such cultures, companies should ensure that employees have career development plans addressing training activities and work experience in possible future roles. Assigning career counsellors to provide personalised attention ensures that employees have realistic plans. Organisations with high employee engagement scores gave counselling sessions at least twice a year; low scores gave sessions less than once a year.

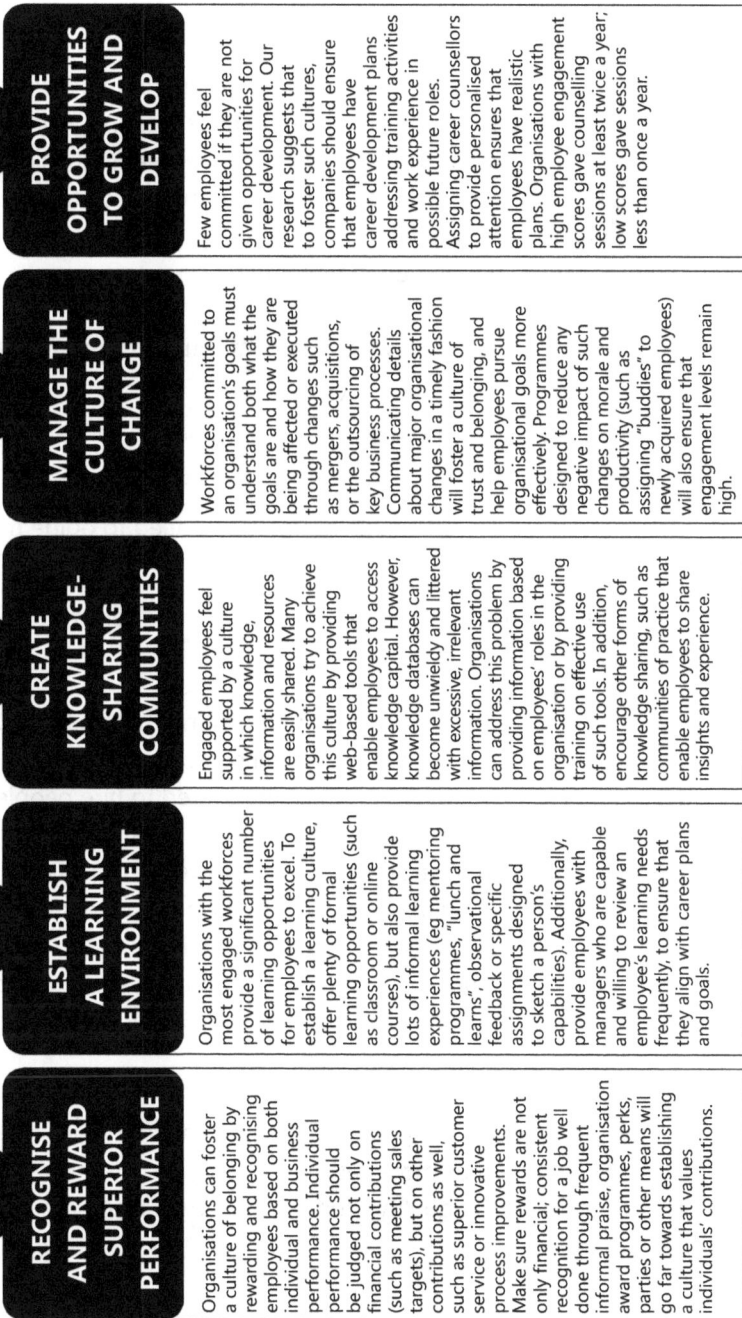

Figure 9: The Five Pillars of Engagement[36]

Key drivers of employee engagement

Achieving employee engagement is about getting employees to think and act like business leaders and about creating a work environment that causes people to perform at exceedingly high levels – a place where employees want to use their discretionary effort on behalf of the organisation. According to our research, the four dimensions to creating engagement are:

- line of sight: I know how what I do contributes to business goals and outcomes;

- involvement: I know I can make decisions which will influence business results;

- share information: I have the information I need to guide my decisions; and

- reward and recognition: I know I'll be rewarded for my contributions.

On the other hand, Development Dimensions International's (DDI) value proposition includes four sequential components. In DDI's model of engagement drivers, organisations need to hire people who fit the job profile, develop leaders with the right skills, and provide support through strong strategies. More specifically, an engaged environment builds loyalty in employees by meeting their personal and practical needs, thereby encouraging them to stay in the organisation. An engaged working environment also leads to greater employee motivation, which can make the distinction from the organisation's competitors.

Finally, long-term benefits appear on the bottom line, which shows that the organisation has more satisfied and loyal customers, increased profits, better quality products or services, and greater growth potential.

TED
Ideas worth spreading

See this Ted Talk for more ideas on hiring: https://
www.ted.com/talks/regina_hartley_why_the_
best_hire_might_not_have_the_perfect_resume

ENGAGEMENT DRIVERS
- Right employees in the right jobs
- Exceptional leadership
- Organisational systems and strategies

WORK ENVIRONMENT
- Aligned effort and strategy
- Empowerment
- Teamwork/collaboration
- Growth and development
- Support and recognition

ORGANISATIONAL SUCCESS
- Satisfied/loyal customers
- Increased retention
- High profits and profitability
- Revenue growth

ENGAGED EMPLOYEES
- Greater loyalty
- Enhanced effort

Figure 10: DDI's engagement value proposition

As seen in the model, organisations can drive engagement by proactively leveraging three sources of influence for change: employees, leaders and organisational systems. These three drivers work together to create an engaged working environment, but the ultimate ownership of engagement rests with the employee.

In order for engagement to occur, organisations must tap into employees' passion, commitment and identification with the organisation. In order to do this, organisations must ensure that the right employee is in the right job. In other words, employees who have the skills to do the job as well as the personal motivation and willingness to do their jobs must be correctly placed in the organisation.

DDI's research drew the following conclusions:

■ Additional studies have shown that changes in leaders' behaviours can have a real impact on employee engagement. Engaging leaders understand that their role is not to take charge of all the decisions – it's about recognition for a job well done, it's about giving people the room and encouragement to grow, it's about being tough when necessary, and it's about holding people accountable for their performance.

■ Organisations need strong systems and strategies that support and foster engagement. Examples of these are hiring, promotion, performance management, recognition, remuneration, training, and career development.

■ Together, these systems provide an organisational foundation upon which to accelerate engagement. A shaky or incomplete foundation will make an organisation's efforts to build engagement more difficult, if not impossible.

The importance of measurement and benchmarks

For over 30 years, the Gallup Organisation has surveyed approximately three million employees in 300,000 work units within companies. This survey consists of 12 questions – called the Q12 – and measures employee engagement on a five-point scale indicating weak or strong agreement. Their results have shown that companies with high Q12 scores experience lower turnover, higher sales growth, enhanced productivity, better customer loyalty, and other manifestations of superior performance.

The following are the 12 questions that the Gallup Organisation uses to measure employee engagement:

■ Do you know what is expected of you at work?

■ Do you have the materials and equipment you need to do your work right?

- At work, do you have the opportunity to do what is best every day?

- In the last seven days, have you received recognition or praise for doing good work?

- Does your supervisor, or someone at work, seem to care about you as a person?

- Is there someone at work who encourages your development?

- At work, do your opinions seem to count?

- Does the mission/purpose of your organisation make you feel your job is important?

- Are your associates (fellow employees) committed to doing quality work?

- Do you have a best friend at work?

- In the last six months, has someone at work talked to you about your progress?

- In the last year, have you had opportunities at work to learn and grow?

Our suggestion is to create an engagement survey and run it in your organisation. The absolute result does not really matter, it is the direction year-on-year that matters. Are you getting better and moving forward?

Conclusion

Remuneration-based retention strategies are critical, but simply throwing money at the problem will not make retention issues go away in the long term. The focus in retention strategies has shifted from a one-size-fits-all approach to customisation. Each employee is motivated by different factors depending on their age, status, career goals, and so on. For this reason, retention strategies must be targeted at individual employees or groups of employees.

In short, why retention is such an issue for organisations is that retaining valued workers helps keep companies successful. When star performers leave, they take their knowledge with them. Organisations need to learn how to engage talent competently to ensure the continuous transfer and encoding of knowledge, so that in the event of knowledge workers leaving, their knowledge is retained by the organisation. Through the successful engagement of knowledge employees, a high level of commitment can be achieved during their tenure at the organisation, thereby maximising the return to the employer as well as the employee.

Now that both rewards and engagement have been discussed in a global context, reward preferences will be discussed.

Summary of main points

- Each country is different, but there are some universal themes.

- Some countries are more advanced in their remuneration management than others but there are some worldwide certainties.

- There is a growing need to link pay to performance.

- Better salary surveys, benchmarking and practices are essential.

Chapter 4

Reward and retention preferences

This chapter covers:

- The African perspective of rewards and retention preferences.

- The multi-dimensional nature of reward.

- The drivers of reward strategies.

- Proactive reward strategies.

- A Total Reward Statement and what this contains.

*The **right** total reward strategy can deliver the **right** amount to a sufficient supply of the **right** people at the **right** time, for the **right** reasons.*
Adapted from Gross and Friedman[37]

Effective reward strategies positively influence employee behaviour by incorporating extrinsic and intrinsic motivators. Employees receive tangible and intangible rewards in return for their performance, while making a meaningful contribution to the organisation. As the organisation succeeds, so does the employee, and vice versa.

The African perspective

What makes the African perspective from a reward and retention point of view different or the same from the rest of the world is a topic of constant debate in our boardrooms and Remuneration Committees. Africa is a huge continent with 52 countries and one cannot generalise across the whole continent, however there are some general truisms that are shared among most countries. The table below sets out a summary of some of the key differences and similarities with the rest of the world.

Table 5: Remuneration and retention differences and similarities – Africa vs. the rest of the world

Differences	Similarities
Most African countries have a "soft" currency (very few countries have a hard currency e.g. Zimbabwe adopted the USD), whereas other jurisdictions have hard currencies.	Most African organisations have Boards and Remuneration or HR Subcommittees that govern remuneration.
Africa has an abundance of unskilled and uneducated labour, with low maths and literacy rates and high unemployment rates; in the US and Europe, people are highly educated.	The structure of reward is similar to other continents, i.e. salary, benefits, short-term and long-term incentive schemes. (Given the few stock exchanges in Africa, the LTI schemes tend to be cash-based and roll over several years.)
Most of Africa is heavily involved in primary production.	Sophisticated remuneration benchmarking surveys/tools are available but not necessarily utilised.
Africa generally has lower pay rates than our more economically developed trading partners.	There is some focus in HR training on remuneration.
Generally speaking, people hang on to their jobs and are very cautious about moving jobs, especially where uncertainty is involved. This necessitates retention for only the very scarcest of skills.	The world famous WorldatWork GRP courses are tutored.
Mobility due to passport and work permit requirements is tougher than throughout the European Union or Americas.	
In Africa there are strong trade unions and heavy government involvement.	Similar legislative and tax frameworks as the rest of the world.

Although much has been copied from developed nations, Africa has a lot to offer in terms of lessons learnt from a variety of situations such as sanctions, hyper-inflation, poor mobility due to tough work permit requirements and generalist skills that are hard to come by. Some of the unique aspects of Africa are set out below, including what was adapted and is working well.

Multi-dimensional construct of reward

The reward arena is fertile ground for confusion, as the term can have different meanings that are derived from varying situations and contexts. It is therefore important to clarify a few related terms based on the most widely-used interpretations. Some elements of a reward system are described as follows:

- *Policies* provide guidelines on managing rewards and include, for example, comparison to market, internal equity versus external equity, the composition of the total reward offering, the role of line managers in decision-making, governance concerning pay decisions, and transparency.

- *Practices or systems* provide for financial and non-financial rewards and outcomes (for example, increases) that can be either performance- or non-performance-orientated.

- *Processes* are concerned with reward, for example, evaluating the relative size of jobs (job evaluation) and assessing individual performance (performance management).

- *Procedures* are followed in order to maintain the reward system and to ensure that it operates efficiently and flexibly and provides value for money.

- *Reward criteria* refer to the bases upon which organisations determine and distribute rewards.

- *Reward strategies* set out what the organisation intends to do in the longer term, for example to develop and implement reward policies, practices and processes to support the achievement of business goals and meet individual needs.

Generally speaking, these are fairly well developed in Africa.

Drivers of reward strategies

Four considerations contribute to making strategic reward and remuneration decisions. These include the:

- organisation's (business) strategy;
- organisation's product life cycle;
- organisation's remuneration policy; and
- employees' reward preferences and needs.

This framework is used extensively when designing reward strategies.

Organisational strategy

The ultimate objective of the total reward strategy is to ensure that the company attracts and retains the right employees, and that it motivates them to do those things that support the business plan while also being legally compliant. Recognition for outstanding achievement is also an important part of the process. The right total reward strategy can deliver the right amount to the right people at the right time, for the right reasons.[38]

The organisational strategy refers to the fundamental direction adopted by the organisation, with the broader organisational strategy giving rise to specific questions at different levels in the organisation. At the executive management level, the question revolves round the kind of business the organisation should be involved in. At the functional level, the question revolves round how the strategy should be implemented in order to achieve the organisational goals. Where remuneration is concerned, the question is whether the existing reward and remuneration strategy will encourage employees to behave in a way that will lead to the achievement of the organisational goals.

Organisations can choose to follow various business strategies; the most commonly used are the innovator strategy, cost-cutter strategy, and the consumer-focused strategy. These strategies require diverse and even contrasting behaviours from employees, so the remuneration strategies should vary in each case. The business that decides to have an innovative business strategy must develop a total reward strategy that will reward innovative behaviour and decisions; the organisation that follows the cost-cutter approach should focus on efficiency and emphasise productivity in the remuneration of employees; and the consumer-focused business strategy should be supported by a remuneration strategy that rewards employee behaviours that ensure customer satisfaction.

The organisational strategy informs the reward strategy, and the reward strategy enables employees to implement the business strategy by giving clear indications of the types of behaviour that will be rewarded. The business plan is used as a point of departure for developing the reward and remuneration strategy. This is followed by an assessment of how well the current TRS supports the objectives of the business. Gaps and any areas that are overfunded are identified, before a pay or remuneration strategy that forms the basis of the TRS is developed. The reward and remuneration philosophy is then updated accordingly and aligned with the business strategy.

The organisation's product life cycle

The industry's or product's growth rate or life cycle stage has a significant impact on the remuneration strategy adopted. Figure 11 shows an example of industry maturity or product life cycle and sets out common organisational strategies that are used in each of these stages.

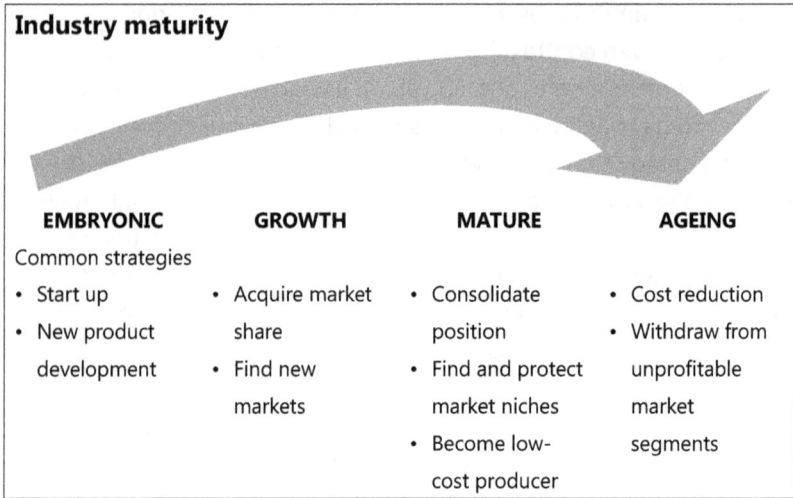

Industry maturity			
EMBRYONIC	**GROWTH**	**MATURE**	**AGEING**
Common strategies			
• Start up • New product development	• Acquire market share • Find new markets	• Consolidate position • Find and protect market niches • Become low-cost producer	• Cost reduction • Withdraw from unprofitable market segments

Figure 11: Industry maturity or product life cycle

Each of these stages has a preferred remuneration strategy attached to it. Table 6 shows the most appropriate remuneration strategy for each stage.

Table 6: Common approaches to reward and remuneration in each life cycle stage

Embryonic	Growth	Mature	Aging
• Less emphasis on salary, benefits and perks • Attention to share options and long-term incentives	• Continued emphasis on long-term incentives, with increasing attention on ways to promote short-term results • Catch up with salary and benefits	• Most attention focused on keeping salary and perks competitive • Reduced concern for long-term incentives • Bonuses oriented to productivity improvement	• Benefits and salary are king • Very little attention given to long-term, growth-oriented incentives

Remuneration policy

The remuneration policy indicates how the remuneration strategy will be implemented. It guides management decisions and should therefore be informative enough to ensure effective decision making, but also be flexible enough to allow for individual differences in pay should this be necessary.

Organisations can choose between several competitive pay policy options. The match policy pays employees' salaries that are similar to those of the competition. This approach ensures that the organisation's remuneration costs are approximately equal to those of the competition, thus its ability to attract and retain talented employees is similar to that of its competitors. When an organisation pays more than its competitors in the market, it follows a lead policy. This approach allows the organisation to attract and retain talented employees, but also increases labour costs. An employer who pays below the current market rate follows a lag policy. This may hinder their ability to attract and retain talent, except when the low basic salary is enhanced with other forms of remuneration such as share options or high-performance bonuses.

Typical content of a remuneration policy:

- Statement of intent and philosophy
- Employee value proposition (EVP)
- Purpose
- Application and scope
- Document control and versions
- Philosophy of guaranteed or fixed pay (GP)
- Philosophy of variable pay (VP)
- Remuneration mix
- Comparative benchmarking

- Links to performance management
- Communication and the extent of transparency allowed
- Annual remuneration reviews
- Remuneration committee scope and guidelines

Components of remuneration structure

Deciding how to develop a reward or remuneration strategy is one of the most important decisions that an organisation has to make. A competitive remuneration policy allows the organisation to use the policy as a tool to attract, but most of all retain, employees and managers. The figure below was developed based on all the different models for total rewards, which are emphasised in the total reward systems section. The figure illustrates the general components of remuneration, for example the concept of Total Guaranteed Package makes for easy cost control, especially for fringe benefits.

Once the mechanisms for determining rates of pay for jobs in an organisation have been settled, the pay or remuneration package should be constructed. As shown in Figure 12, the payment of an individual will be made up of fixed (or guaranteed) pay elements and variable pay elements. **Fixed or guaranteed pay elements** are those that make up the regular weekly or monthly payment to the individual, and do not vary other than in exceptional circumstances. These include basic salary and employee benefits. **Variable pay elements** can be adapted by either the employer or the employee,[39] and include short-term and long-term incentives.

- **Incentives**

    Short-term incentives (STIs) are defined as incentives that are applicable for up to one year, such as **incentive targets**, **discretionary bonuses** and **profit shares**, and are tied to the performance of the company, team and/or individual. An **incentive target** is a bonus that is typically related to the achievement of a financial target such as turnover or profit, as well as other objectives. The **incentive bonus** is typically a percentage of the total guaranteed package, while the **discretionary bonus** is a discretionary amount that bears some relationship to the individual's performance. **Profit share** is a predetermined percentage of the organisation's profits, which is usually also dependent on the achievement of other objectives. **Long-term incentives (LTIs)** refer to incentives that are applicable for over one year, such as a share option scheme, share grant scheme, share purchase scheme, or long-term cash incentive scheme. In pictorial format, the various forms of pay can be represented as follows:

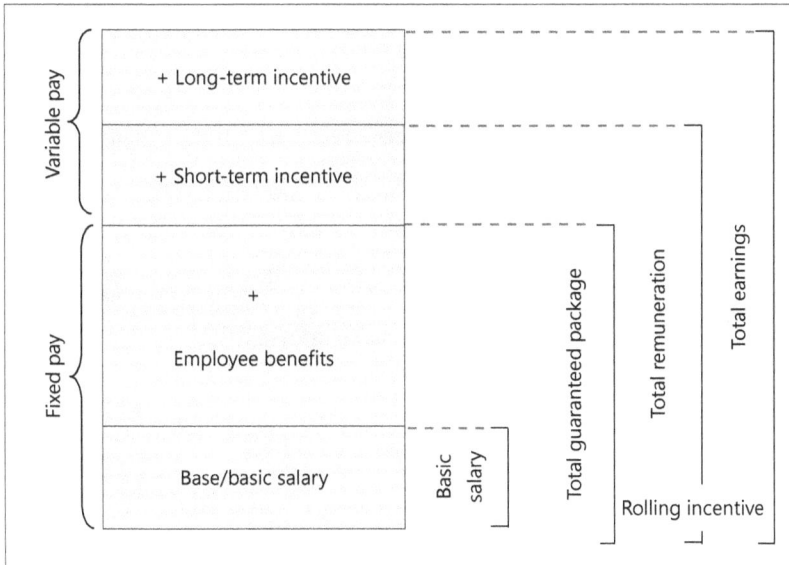

Variable pay
{ + Long-term incentive
+ Short-term incentive

Fixed pay
{ +
Employee benefits
Base/basic salary

Basic salary
Total guaranteed package
Total remuneration
Total earnings
Rolling incentive

Figure 12: Typical elements of remuneration[40]

Individual incentives reward individual performance; sales commissions and once-off bonuses are commonly used individual incentive methods. **Team incentives** focus on the performance of a work group or team. **Gain-sharing plans** are examples of a team incentive that is used, for example, when an employee team achieves specific goals such as reducing waste, reducing accident rates or improving productivity. **Profit-sharing schemes** are commonly implemented at executive level or business unit level. **Organisational incentive** and employee share ownership schemes reward employees based on the performance of the entire organisation.

The best-of-breed organisations use both short-term and long-term incentives in their remuneration mix. The primary purpose of this is that it encourages the long-term viability of the company, and executives are encouraged not to harm the company for short-term gains, because they would have too much to lose in the long term. A well-designed 'total earnings' scheme should prevent this from happening.[41]

The link between the performance management system and remuneration is most commonly experienced in three ways. The higher the performance score:

- the higher the fixed pay increase;
- the greater the slice of the STI pie relative to the pool; and
- the greater the likelihood of receiving a larger amount of the share scheme pool and share top-ups.

TED Ideas worth spreading

See this Ted Talk for more information: https://www.ted.com/talks/dan_pink_on_motivation

Benefits

Benefits (fringe benefits) are indirect remuneration that employees receive because they belong to the workforce of an organisation. These tend to be more common in emerging markets, and in some countries the tax treatment is still favourable towards them. As shown in the table below, these may be either cash or non-cash additions to an employee's pay and must be taken into account when calculating the total package.

Table 7: Examples of cash and non-cash benefits

Examples of cash benefits	Examples of non-cash benefits
• Car allowance • Entertainment allowance • Housing subsidy • Professional fees • Cell phone allowance	• Vacation leave • Sick leave • Pension/provident fund contribution • Medical contribution • Group life assurance • Accident insurance • Housing loan • Educational assistance • Travel abroad

See the following Ted Talk regarding the importance of time off: https://www.ted.com/talks/stefan_sagmeister_the_power_of_time_off

Where trade unions are recognised, any changes to conditions of employment must be negotiated with them. Sometimes, organisations are subject to regulations through bargaining councils, which means that their remuneration practices are prescribed by industry-specific needs. It is unlikely that an application for exemption regarding a total package structure would be successful.

From Figure 12 it can be observed that when basic pay (1) and fringe benefits (2) are combined, this provides the employee with guaranteed remuneration. A combination of short-term incentives and long-term incentives will provide the employee with variable pay. The relationship between guaranteed pay and variable pay is referred to as the remuneration mix. Generally in Africa, the variable pay portion is not as generous as in the rest of the world.

Remuneration options for retention

Remuneration alone cannot lead to a successful retention strategy; 21st Century research suggests that it is only 25% of the stay decision. The other 75% is inspirational leadership, great culture, great career, great workplace and great performance feedback. Market trends on the remuneration options are set out below. This gives an indication of the 25% "ticket to the game".

The most common remuneration approaches to retention include:

- Market stance: Organisations using this strategy pitch their guaranteed package at the upper quartile (Q3) of the market for key or scarce resources. Sometimes a different pay scale is created for specific job families, for example, engineering.

- Restraint-of-trade payments: These payments are often one to five times the annual total guaranteed package. Conditions are attached to the payment, which is fully taxable in the employee's hands and deductible by the employer over the period of restraint. When enforcing the restraint, the courts look at how severe the restraint is in terms of area, time and damage. Restraints that are unreasonable or too onerous are often not enforced.

- Sign-on bonus/Retention bonus: This is a relatively new entrant to the African market. A bonus is promised when an employee joins an organisation (signs on). Practices differ somewhat, but the two most common approaches are to:

  - pay the bonus on day one, and the employee has to repay it if he or she leaves within a period of time, often one to three years; or

  - promise the bonus in, say, two to three years, on the condition that the employee stays and accomplishes certain performance targets.

These bonuses are fully taxable in the employee's hands when received and fully deductible in the company's hands when paid. The quanta are often in the order of one to three times the annual guaranteed package.

Sign-on loans

In this instance, the employee is guaranteed a loan and the debt is written off if the employee is still at the company after a set period of time, for example, three years. There are tax implications up front, as it is not taxable and not deductible. There is fringe benefit tax if the interest on the loan is less than the prescribed rate, and it is taxable in the employee's hands when the debt is written off. Deductibility is uncertain in the employer's hands since it was never included in "income" (and taxed). Deductibility would hinge on whether it is in the production of income.

Rolling or banking of bonus incentives earned

This is a popular approach for non-listed organisations and becoming more popular with all organisations because of its ease and efficacy. Typically, organisations will target a guaranteed pay to variable pay ratio based on salary surveys and niche benchmarking. For example, consider the market data for a CEO in a business of similar size and complexity:

Position	Median GP	Median STI	Median LTI
CEO	1,000,000	500,000	750,000

An incentive bonus scheme is designed where the bonus pay-out for achievement is 1,250,000 (500,000 STI and 750,000 LTI quanta). This is then paid out over, say, three years, typically in the following ratios:

- 50% in year one, 30% in year two and 20% in year three (provided still in the organisation's employ).

- 34% in year one, 33% in year two, and 33% in year three (provided still in the organisation's employ).

On payment, this is fully taxable in the employee's hands and deductible in the organisation's hands. A major advantage of this approach is that it links the incentive targets to the organisation's strategy and line of sight.

Flexibility

The employment contract is characterised by mass customisation of remuneration, benefits, employment conditions, working hours, leave, and supplementary business-related expenditure. Work-life balance and catering for the specific needs of the generations (Veterans, Baby Boomers, Generations X and Y) is growing in importance. High-performing organisations have grasped the "administrative nettle" in order to facilitate retention.

Post-retirement benefits

This approach is more effective for those employees close to retirement. One could consider retirement at 60 years of age, and the organisation elects to continue paying into their retirement and medical funds until, say, the employee is 65 years of age. The value of employer contributions to these funds on behalf of the ex-employee would be taxable as a benefit in the retired employee's hands, while they should be deductible by the employer.

Group-wide bonus with car

In this instance, organisations typically select a single measure or factor that triggers the bonus pay-out, for example, "sales" in a retail organisation and "on-time arrivals and departures" in an airline. If the target is met, a nominal bonus is paid of, say, 100. Should the target be hit for six months in a row and the employee has not been absent once, he or she qualifies for a ticket for the draw of, say, a small car. All employees receive the same amount of 100, and all eligible employees have a shot at winning the car. This scheme is particularly effective in improving an important measure to the organisation and creating teamwork, and in our experience is relatively cheap. Both the

100 and the value of the car would be taxable in the employee's hands and deductible by the employer, assuming that the employer purchased the car at full value.

■ **Long-term incentives (LTI)**

A popular approach is a combination of various approaches, for example, a restraint of trade and rolling incentives that use cash, full shares and share appreciation schemes. Trends in this area include:

☐ LTIs without performance conditions (RSUs – Restricted Share Units) with a two to three year vesting period;

☐ companies using deferrals on their STIs which are an inherent retention measure; and

☐ companies moving towards longer vesting periods on Performance Share Units (PSUs), which addresses both the retention issue and ensures sustainable performance over the long term.

■ **Short-term incentives (STI)**

The global trend for the past ten years has been to ratchet up the variable pay portion in the remuneration mix. This ties the onerous salary and wage bill to the fortunes of the business and drives awareness of the strategy. Well-designed schemes motivate and retain, however organisations need to be aware that the life span of STIs is no more than three to five years, and should be reviewed regularly as the strategy changes. STI awards are generally taxable in the employee's hands and deductible by the employer.

■ **Further trends**

Retention tools that would address a 'special' group (typically around 5% of the work force) and the criteria to identify them have to be sorted out first and then consistently applied, e.g. cash retention awards linked to a work back period. In South Africa you can expect the recipients to pay back the gross amount if they leave before the end of the retention period, as there is a dispensation in the Tax Act for them to then engage with SARS to get the tax on the award back with their next tax return. It is financially quite punitive so it is very effective, however you do not want to end up being stuck with someone who turned into a sour lemon, hence the criteria being critical.

Quick tip:

Motivate employees by means of an incentivised travel programme!

■ Deferred remuneration

The deferred remuneration approach was popular 15 years ago, fell out of favour, and is back again. Typically, the organisation buys an endowment policy for, say, five to ten years, and cedes this to the employee at the end of this period. Alternatively, employees elect not to take the bonus and instead put the money into a policy, and the employer matches the contribution Rand for Rand.

Unfortunately, there is no silver bullet or rabbit that can be pulled out of the hat. Strategies and trends vary, thus the most appropriate solution should be selected. Once the remuneration ticket is in place, one should consider other forms of retention. Inspirational leadership is a very important ingredient, and often leads to engaged employees.

The case for proactive reward and retention strategies

The loss of high quality employees as well as replacement strategies can be believed to have an economic impact on any organisation. The decision of an employee to stay or leave is potentially costly, often between half to two times the annual salary of the incumbent. Advertising, recruitment, and orientation and training courses for new employees, as well as decreased morale and productivity, are all factors that need to be considered. It is thus vital that when organisations attain the appropriately skilled employees, they implement retention strategies to prevent them from leaving. It can be noted that an Employee Value Proposition (EVP) is a retention strategy that is specific and unique to each organisation. In order for an organisation to retain employees to perform optimally, it must match its rewards to its employees' preferences.

There are several types of labour turnover, namely:

- Involuntary turnover – this is where staff leaves the organisation involuntarily, i.e. not of their own free will. Examples of this are death or retrenchment.
- Voluntary turnover – this is where staff members leave of their own accord.

Organisations need a healthy balance of the two; the average labour turnover is approximately 12%, i.e. about 12 out of every 100 employees leave their organisation each year.

People decide to switch jobs for a wide variety of reasons. New blood is a good thing, but a constant turnover is detrimental to performance, morale and overall sustainability. Some reasons are related to personal and life changes and completely unrelated to the job itself, so a business cannot expect to impact or change all departures, although with workers switching jobs roughly every 4.4 years, businesses do need to be focused on the aspects of employee retention they can influence. The need for organisations to adopt a purposeful attraction and retention strategy is driven by the changing marketplace in Africa, and it is becoming an imperative for organisations to introduce effective staff attraction and retention tactics.

Remuneration implications

So what are the remuneration implications for retention strategies? A shift in the organisation's mindset may involve some of the following points; most African organisations have started moving down several of these roads:

- Pay for **contributions or outputs** rather than job duty adherence or service.
- Reward requires **competence** development and application.
- Rely on **performance-related pay** as a means of conveying messages about organisational values, critical success factors and how people are expected to contribute.
- Include both **input** (competence) and **output** (results) in performance reviews.
- Introduce robust pay structures where lateral development as well as acquisition and use of skills are rewarded.
- Develop **team reward** systems which support flexible work practices, multi-skilling and team work.
- Introduce gain-sharing, profit-sharing or any bonus scheme that **shares the added value** of employee efforts.
- **Communicate** reward innovations to employees.
- **Involve**, as far as practical, employees in the design of reward processes.
- Provide **training** to everyone on the application and implications of the reward policies and practices.

These implications have far reaching outcomes for the HR strategy; high performing organisations adopt these as the minimum standard.

Total Reward Statements

Total rewards is a term that has been used by HR professionals for over 10 years to describe the concept of several employment factors such as remuneration, benefits, performance, recognition, career and work-life amenities that can be strategically applied to deliver desired employee attraction, motivation and retention. **It is one of the quickest and cheapest wins to boost retention and make employees realise the value of what it costs the company to keep them**. Africa is well on the way to producing Total Reward Statements for all employees at least once a year. Set out below is a typical explanation and implementation process used on the continent.

Total Reward Statement defined

A Total Reward Statement (TRS) provides employees with a personalised document that communicates the overall value of their financial rewards; it monetises everything received by the employee. A TRS can also be used to reinforce the communication of less tangible benefits such as work-life programmes, learning and development, and flexible work arrangements.

What they contain

In order to provide individuals with a thorough and comprehensive visibility of their overall reward package, a TRS has to contain details of both the tangible and intangible rewards offered by the business, clearly including the perks offered under a flexible, and eventually voluntary, benefits programme. In addition to fixed and variable pay, each TRS thus needs to contain details about pensions, private medical insurance, life assurance, share schemes, company cars, fuel, car insurance, taxes related to car possession/use (where applicable), laptops, mobile phones, gym memberships, subsidised canteens, luncheon vouchers and anything else that may be subsidised or costs the employer money.

To whom are they addressed?

Some organisations used to prepare a TRS just for managerial and executive positions, or more generally for those individuals they had more interest in retaining.

However, line managers often underestimate the value of their direct reports' reward packages; staff often compare their basic salaries with those offered by their competitors, rather than considering and focusing on the overall reward package's value offered by their current employer.

The benefit organisations can derive from giving evidence of the perks offered to all of their staff cannot be emphasised enough. It can be priceless in terms of developing, strengthening and endorsing employer branding, as well as helping employers to retain staff.

However, if line managers do not understand the mechanics and the way a total reward package is designed and operated, they will not clearly be able to understand the value of their own reward package, let alone be able to explain the meaning of this to their direct reports.

Why produce Total Reward Statements?

Set out below are some of the reasons organisations produce Total Reward Statements for staff:

- To attract, motivate and retain employees.
- To reinforce their brand and set them apart from other organisations.
- To raise awareness and appreciation by focusing attention on the benefits the organisation offers.
- To reduce the cost of benefits administration by providing an employee a self-service tool that results in fewer phone calls, thereby enabling HR to focus more on strategic issues.

On a more practical note, everyone benefits from fully understanding exactly what the total cost of reward is.

Who will benefit from Total Reward Statements?

The trend to Total Reward Statements is driven by the many benefits to both employer and employee. Some of the beneficiaries of these statements include:

- Organisations that are cash-constrained, which could become more competitive by selling the value of intangible rewards or benefits those employees find difficult to value.

- Organisations that are experiencing staff turnover due to perceived weakness/lack of desired reward elements.

- Organisations that have large numbers of employees across multi-national operations; economies of scale can be realised by producing statements in bulk.

- Organisations that are able to thoroughly identify all the benefits and reward design aspects across the geographical areas concerned. Having recourse to statements will also help corporations to ascertain which sources of data can make benefits management more straightforward in each of the countries concerned.

- Employees who are educated and informed about their reward packages and have the tools to assist them with their own financial planning think about their packages in an integrated way.

When should employers avoid Total Reward Statements?

It is strongly suggested not to introduce TRSes when the data are unreliable. Another case when businesses may find it more appropriate to avoid issuing TRSes is after having completed the process of acquiring, or merging with, other organisations. Since the benefits structures and payroll systems of the businesses concerned could be different, it may be better to collect and ensure offerings are comparable before issuing TRSes.

Employers also tend to avoid introducing TRSes when they actually offer very little in addition to basic salary or when take-up rates of the current offering is rather low.

With what frequency should Total Reward Statements be disseminated?

An organisation may provide individualised information on a one time basis or in other cases annually to ensure that their employees have a complete picture of the total value of being employed at the organisation. This statement could be in printed or in electronic format, but having it printed allows it to be shared with family outside the workplace. In most cases, the HR department is partly responsible for the assembly and distribution of these documents.

What is the best way to communicate about Total Reward Statements?

When considering introducing TRSes, one of the first decisions employers need to make is how they will convey the desired information. Organisations whose employees have access to a computer may decide to allow them to use the corporate intranet or a dedicated website specific to the organisation.

Some organisations produce statements only for executives and senior managers, in order to emphasise and stress the exclusivity of the document and the quality of the benefits offered. Usually TRSes are printed on superior thick paper and packed into expensive cases, which helps to catch a manager's attention.

Technological developments have been beneficial to the implementation of TRSes. Online statements can clearly provide a more intriguing and immediate overview of the reward package received by each employee, who, if required, can by means of pop-ups and additional links access further information or explanations about the statements' content. The figure below shows an example of a TRS from a numbers point of view. Typically there is a lot more information in the statement.

Your personal details:

Employee number: 000001

Date of birth: 01/01/1960

Date you joined: 01/01/2000

John your total reward is: **1,070,420.54**

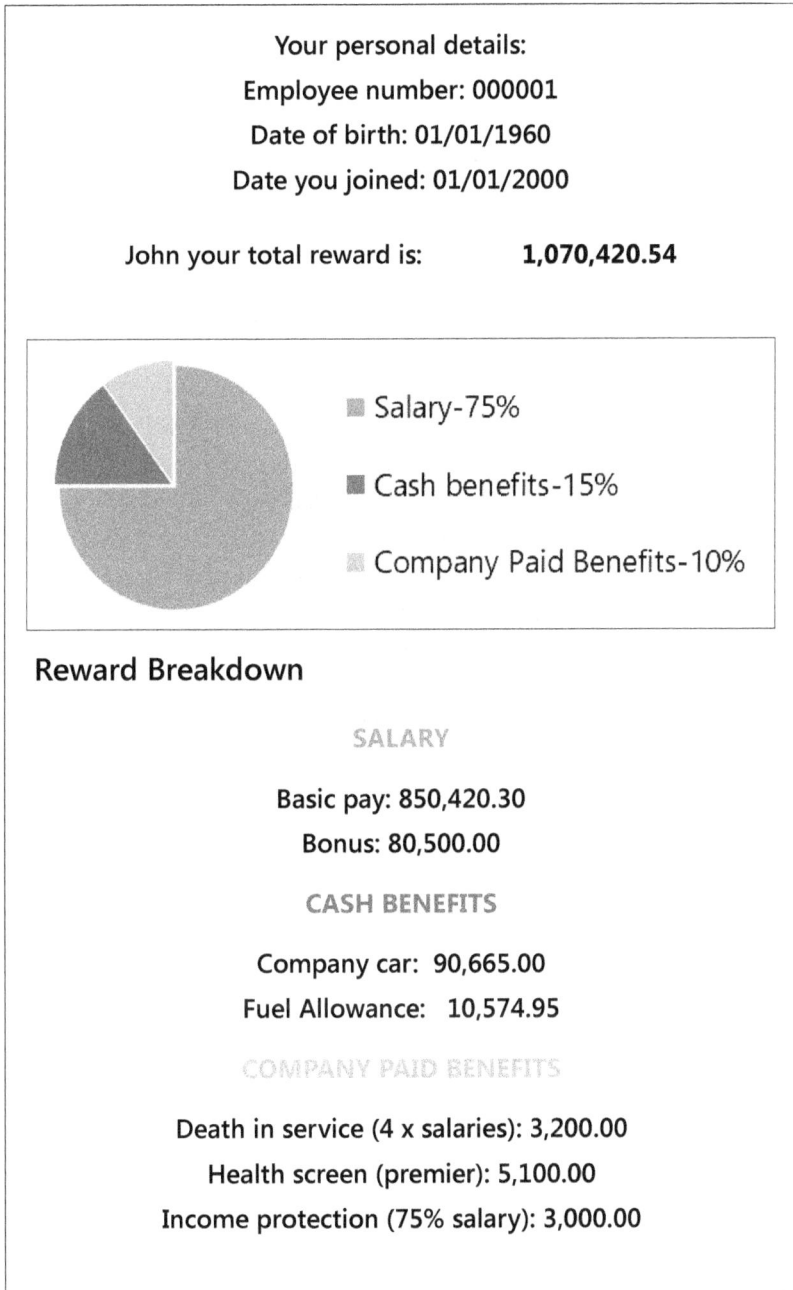

Salary-75%

Cash benefits-15%

Company Paid Benefits-10%

Reward Breakdown

SALARY

Basic pay: 850,420.30

Bonus: 80,500.00

CASH BENEFITS

Company car: 90,665.00

Fuel Allowance: 10,574.95

COMPANY PAID BENEFITS

Death in service (4 x salaries): 3,200.00

Health screen (premier): 5,100.00

Income protection (75% salary): 3,000.00

Figure 13: An example of a Total Rewards Statement

Conclusion

In my view, employees join companies and leave bosses, thus the best spend may well be on the training and development of bosses to be better and more inspiring leaders. It is important to remember that the retention of key staff cannot be guaranteed by an increase in remuneration levels, and should rather be approached by adopting a multi-pronged attraction and retention philosophy.

Employees work for an organisation out of choice, not out of obligation. In order to effectively attract, retain and develop talent, it becomes necessary for organisations to utilise the mechanisms outlined throughout this chapter. The skills present in an organisation should be regarded as tools to sculpt the workforce and consequently enrich the organisation. Strategies and trends change over time, and the most appropriate solution should be selected based on the needs of your organisation.

No doubt there are many other employee retention strategies for engaging and retaining employees, however these tips should serve as a good start. Be transparent, have a clear employee value proposition, communicate with employees early and often, know what they want and what you want, and understand what motivates them.

Not only do reward preferences differ among continents or even countries, they differ according to different generations. This will be discussed in the next chapter.

Summary

Summary
☐ —
☐ —
☐ —

Summary of main points

- A reward strategy is an important component of the retention of talent, but is not sufficient on its own to secure employee retention.

- The total rewards package shows absolutely everything that is a cost to the employer in one statement.

- Total rewards differ in each country and must be designed to fit the preferences of employees so that they are enticed to remain at the organisation.

Chapter 5

Total rewards and the employee value proposition (EVP)

> **This chapter covers:**
>
> ■ The link between EVP, total rewards and retention.
>
> ■ Case study examples demonstrating market practice.

Introduction

"What's in it for me?" is probably the simplest description of the Employee Value Proposition (EVP). Minchington[42] defined an EVP more broadly as a set of associations and offerings provided by an organisation in return for the skills, capabilities and experiences an employee brings to the organisation. According to the Corporate Leadership Council[43], an EVP is the total employment experience and therefore the differentiated total compelling employment offer.

Although many organisations are not currently focused on the attraction and retention of key talent due to the recent recession, it remains important for organisations to have a unique, relevant and compelling EVP that acts as a key driver of talent attraction, engagement and retention in the long term. The EVP should identify the unique people policies, processes and programmes that demonstrate the organisation's commitment to, for example, employee growth, management development, ongoing employee recognition, community service, etc. The EVP contains the reasons why employees will choose to commit themselves to a specific organisation.[44]

The EVP is an employee-centred approach that is aligned to integrated talent management strategies. An organisation's EVP is typically informed by existing employees as well as prospective employees, therefore an organisation needs to understand what talent it needs to attract and retain currently as well as in the future, and how it will differentiate its offering in the labour markets. The challenge for organisations is thus to:

- clearly articulate the EVP and package or brand it (also referred to as employer branding);

- link the proposition to business strategy, talent needs and business results; and

- integrate the different components of the EVP with financial and non-financial reward elements.

EVP and total rewards

The term EVP is often incorrectly used in an interchangeable manner with the concept of total rewards, creating confusion in terms of what EVP stands for versus what total rewards refers to. Although rewards are critical to an organisation's EVP, they are only a subset of the EVP. Different authors have different opinions about what components should be included in the ambit of an organisation's EVP, for example, Lamoureux[45] stated that the key components of the EVP include:

- **remuneration** - salary, incentives, cash recognition, pay process;

- **benefits** – healthcare, retirement, insurances, recognition programmes;

- **affiliation** – work environment, trust, transparency, organisational commitment;

- **career** – advancement opportunities, personal growth and development, training, job security; and

- **work content** – challenge, autonomy, meaningfulness, variety.

Towers Perrin[46] explained that the EVP complements total rewards by adding components such as market benchmarking, leadership research and organisational performance. Black[47], meanwhile, identified four components that form the foundation of an organisation's EVP, namely:

- strong leadership;

- organisational reputation, which includes reputation, culture, contribution to the community and the world, stability and core values;

- interesting and compelling job and career opportunities; and

- tangible and intangible rewards.

The 21st Century pay solution group uses the following diagram to explain the concept of an EVP:

Remuneration	Performance feedback	Career & development	Work environment	Inspirational leadership
• **Ticket to the game** • **Has to be right** • **Flexible** • **Internal & external equity**	• How am I doing? • Development • Control over performance • Link to pay	• I know where I am going • Growth of portable skills • Vertical and horizontal	• Stimulating • Telecommuting • Work-life balance • HR policies	• Leading and managing • Training • Development • Dual career paths
Attract	**Motivate**	**Retain**	**Enjoy**	**Enthuse Inspire**

Figure 14: Employee Value Proposition

Rewards are therefore clearly a component that contributes to the overall EVP, but the EVP also includes the intangible experience and reputation of the organisation as well as, *inter alia*, culture, organisational brand and success, transformation initiatives, environmental concern and job security.[48]

Some examples of EVPs

Organisations clearly differentiate themselves in terms of their EVPs. Some examples of how organisations define their EVPs are listed below:

- Working at **Starbucks**[49] is a lot like working with your friends. We understand, respect, appreciate and include different people. And we believe in keeping each other informed, so our senior leaders regularly hold Open Forum events to answer your questions. Starbucks refers to their EVP as "Your Special Blend", which includes a wide range of perquisites if one works for the organisation i.e.:

  □ Competitive pay
  □ Insurance: medical, prescription drug, dental, vision, life, disability
  □ Bonuses
  □ Paid time off
  □ Retirement savings plan
  □ Equity in the form of Starbucks stock and discounted stock purchase plan
  □ Adoption assistance
  □ Domestic partner benefits
  □ Emergency financial aid
  □ Referral and support resources for child and elder care
  □ *A free pound of coffee each week*

- At **Google**, the EVP includes a culture that drives a fun place to work, subsidised broadband for all employees, pool tables in the tea room, on-site dental care, free t-shirts twice a week, free meals and the opportunity to bring your dog to work.

- **Nedbank's** employer brand of "great things begin with great people" is supported by the nine elements of the Nedbank EVP, namely:

  □ Performance is recognised and rewarded
  □ An organisation that truly cares

- A place where you can thrive
- We have a community of leaders with a clear vision
- A values-based organisation with a high-performance culture
- An organisation that is proudly South African
- People that are bright and amazing to work with
- A role with a sense of purpose and true value add
- People's individual needs are respected

Allstate includes three components in their EVP:

- A company that is innovative, successful and community minded
- Leaders who inspire, build trust and empower employees to achieve optimal performance
- An environment where employees feel valued and rewarded

The **Sasol** EVP consists of the following five themes:

- Flexible work practices
- Reward and benefits
- Learning and development and career opportunities
- Organisational reputation and leadership
- Relationship with my line manager

The **Sodexo** EVP themes are summarised as follows:

- We care about our employees in the same way that we care about our clients and we strive to provide each and every employee with a wide range of professional and personal opportunities to improve the quality of their daily life.
- Our employees are able to develop their careers both locally and globally across all of our service areas. They have the flexibility to align the pace of their career with their various life stages.
- By living the Sodexo values and ethical principles, and actively fostering diversity and inclusion, our people make Sodexo a company of the future.

Conclusion

An EVP is a unique and proprietary way in which organisations attract, retain and motivate employees. Increasingly, more organisations are citing "culture" as a challenge to attract and retain talent, therefore forward-thinking organisations are revisiting their employee value propositions to ensure that the components that make up their EVPs remain relevant and in step with what employees require when they search for an organisation to work for. Organisations have also started to differentiate their EVPs on the basis of the different needs that employees have in the generational segments. For example, career opportunities are much more important for younger employees than older employees, therefore a stronger emphasis is placed on career opportunities when organisations recruit for younger employees. The CLC[50] has also found that engineering and research employees place a premium on innovative work, IT employees place a premium on organisational technology, and marketing employees value product brand awareness. These areas of interest can be very effectively integrated into an organisation's EVP, with minor adjustments for different areas of the workforce.

The integration of total rewards and an EVP is key to obtaining the optimal effectiveness of both systems. By using an EVP effectively, organisations distinguish themselves in the marketplace to both attract and retain critically skilled employees. In order to do this, organisations should communicate to both potential and current employees a compelling and unique EVP, of which total rewards is a critical part.

Summary of main points

■ Employers should ask themselves – why would anyone want to come and work here, as opposed to anywhere else? The answer is the start of articulating the EVP for that employer, which in turn will assist with employee retention.

■ The EVP and total rewards are often used interchangeably, but the EVP is much broader and all encompassing.

Chapter 6

Retention of different generations

....

> **This chapter covers:**
>
> ■ The impact on retention on different generations.
>
> ■ The importance of considering generational components in a reward and retention strategy.

Over the last few years, organisations have had difficulty dealing with the changing financial setting that has challenged conventional reward procedures and plans. A complete understanding of reward packages is needed, as total rewards include intrinsic and extrinsic factors. An in-depth investigation of the reward packages and factors influencing them is essential, as these elements have a key impact on performance, job satisfaction and retaining high calibre talent with significant abilities to promote organisational effectiveness. More specifically, research has shown that the different types of rewards employers offer to employees affect the recruitment and retention of top talent.

....

Reward and generations

....

Employers should recognise the significance of financial and non-financial rewards, as reward practices can work for one organisation but not necessarily for another, depending on the needs of the employees within the organisation and the business strategy.

Although some may argue that there are no distinct generations and different preferences, but rather individual life-cycle and career stages, there is growing support for Generation Theory as a proxy for other empirically researched theories. A study conducted in 2017 with 303 participants from South African organisations revealed the following Top 7 retention preferences among the different generations:

Table 8: Top 7 retention preferences among different generations

Rated as important	Generation Y (<31)	Generation X (32-47)	Baby Boomers and Veterans (47+)
1st	Performance management and recognition	Performance management and recognition	Remuneration
2nd	Development and career opportunities	Development and career opportunities	Performance management and recognition
3rd	Benefits and safety	Remuneration	Benefits and safety
4th	Remuneration	Benefits and safety	Development and career opportunities
5th	Work-life balance	Communication work enabler	Communication work enabler
6th	Communication work enabler	Work-life balance	Work-life balance
7th	Life convenience	Life convenience	Life convenience

Quick tip:

Hiring a graduate increases the chances of retention.

Most organisations find that hiring someone fresh out of college increases the likelihood of the individual staying there longer, although you have to offer them what they are looking for.

It can be deduced that for Baby Boomers and Veterans, remuneration, performance management and recognition and benefits and safety are the top three components that will make them stay at their respective organisations, as they place a high value on hard work, obeying the rules, dedication and military principles. The rating of the benefits and safety subscale as the third most important subscale was surprising as it was expected that the preference for this reward would increase as an employee gets older.

Generation X is willing to develop their skill sets and take on challenges, and is perceived as being very adaptive in this changing business world. Performance management and recognition, development and career opportunities and remuneration are important to them. They are excellent at multi-tasking and working on projects simultaneously, and place a high value on work-life balance. Generation X views their jobs as temporary and see themselves as free agents.

While Generation Y places an emphasis on performance management and recognition, development and career opportunities and benefits and safety round out their top three. Generation Y favours teamwork and chooses to follow orders to the extent that they have flexi-hours in which they can successfully complete their tasks in their own way. This generation uses information channels to familiarise themselves with the environment and has a constant need for knowledge. Generation Y also seeks challenges and enjoys learning and development opportunities, as they are open-minded and goal-orientated in order to grow in their respective careers.

Conclusion

The study of total reward, and specifically different generational groups' perceptions regarding this field, is ever changing. Talent management is a comprehensive, multi-dimensional concept with a myriad of perceptions that influences its effectiveness. It holds the potential to influence talent retention amongst different generations of employees, and therefore confirms the proposition that talent can make organisations perform to their true potential. This ability of talent management to unlock capital has been the driving force behind it becoming a popular field of study.

The key to attracting, and most importantly retaining, excellent employees is based on the creation of an improved diverse total reward model that is a vital foundation for the EVP.

Summary of main points

■ The key to attracting, and most of all retaining, excellent employees is based on improved diverse total reward models. These have to be adapted to the reward preferences of each generation.

■ A TRS should reflect the monetised portion of every single cost of employing someone. That way, employees can make informed decisions around their intentions to stay or leave.

■ Having complete information about procedural fairness (how one's pay is set) and distributive justice (the amount one earns), together with meaningful work and a great boss, is more than likely going to retain top talent.

Endnotes

1   United Nations Educational, Scientific and Cultural Organization (UNESCO). 2010. *Women's and Girls' Access to and Participation in Science and Technology*. Retrieved from: http://www.un.org/womenwatch/daw/egm/gst_2010/UNESCO-BP.2-EGM-ST.pdf.

2   Singh, N. 2 January 2017. India Inc curtails post-maternity attrition. Mumbai edition: *The Economic Times*. Retrieved from: https://economictimes.indiatimes.com/jobs/india-inc-curtails-post-maternity-attrition/articleshow/56289061.cms?utm_source=contentofinterest&utm_medium=text&utm_campaign=cppst

3   Craig, D. 2013. *Developing a Retention Strategy – A Case Study*. Retrieved from: http://www.humancapitalreview.org/content/default.asp?Article_ID=1284

4   Watson Wyatt. 2008-9. *Continuous Engagement: The Key to Unlocking the Value of Your People During Tough Times. Work Europe Survey*.

5   Wellins, R.S., Bernthal, P. and Phelps, M. 2005. *Employee Engagement: the key to realising competitive advantage*. Retrieved from: www.ddiworld.com/pdf/ddi_employee engagement_mg.pdf.

6   Dairy Australia. 2016. *Retention strategies*. Retrieved from: http://www.thepeopleindairy.org.au/individual-performance/retention-strategies.htm

7   Allen, D.G. 2008. *Retaining talent: A guide to analyzing and managing employee turnover*. Alexandra, VA: SHRM Foundation.

8   Cascio, W.F. 2010. *Managing Human Resources: Productivity, Quality of Work Life, Profits* (8th ed.). Burr Ridge, IL: Richard D. Irwin.

9   O'Connell, M. and Kung, M.C. 2007. The cost of employee turnover. *Industrial Management*, 49(1), 14-19.

10 Minton-Eversole, T. 2012. *SHRM poll: Some industries shaking off recession woes*. Retrieved from: https://blog.shrm.org/trends/shrm-poll-some-industries-shaking-off-recession-woes

11 Scott, D., McMullen, T. and Royal, M. 2012. *Retention of Key Talent and the Role of Rewards*. Retrieved from: https://www.worldatwork.org/docs/research-and-surveys/survey-brief-retention-of-keytalent-and-the-role-of-rewards.pdf

12 WorldatWork Conference. 2012. *The Role of Reward in Retaining Key Talent*. Retrieved from: https://www.slideshare.net/HayGroup/mcmullen-role-of-reward-in-retaining-key-talent?from_action=save

13 Scott, K.D., McMullen, T.D. and Nolan, J. 2005. Taking control of your counter-offer environment. *WorldatWork Journal*, 14(1), 25-41.

14 Scott, McMullen & Royal, 2012. Refer endnote 11.

15 Trevisan, L.M., Veloso, E.F.R., da Silva, R.C., Dutra, J.S. and Fischer, A.L. 2014. Talent retention strategies in different organizational contexts and intention of talent to remain in the company. *Journal on Innovation and Sustainability*, 5(1), 49–61.

16 Paul, G.W. and Berry, D.M. 2013. The importance of executive leadership in creating a postmerged organisational culture conducive to effective performance management. *SA Journal of Human Resource Management*, 11(1), 1–15.

17 Kaiser, R.B. and Hogan, R. 2010. How to (and how not to) assess the integrity of managers. *Consulting Psychology Journal: Practice and Research*, 62(4), 216–234.

18 Chatman, J.A. and Cha, S.E. 2003. Leading by leveraging culture. *California Management Review*, 45(4), 20–33.

19 Grojean, M.W., Resick, C.J., Dickson, M.W. and Smith, D.B. 2004. Leaders, values, and organizational climate: Examining leadership strategies for establishing an organizational climate regarding ethics. *Journal of Business Ethics*, 55(3), 223–241.

20 Ramlall, S. 2004. A review of employee motivation theories and their implications for employee retention within organizations. *Journal of American Academy of Business*, 5, 52–64.

21 Messmer, B.M. 2004. Retaining your top performers. *Strategic Finance*, 85(10), 11–13.

22 Ryan, R. 2010. Hanging onto high potentials. *Accounting Today*, 24(10), 38.

23 Allen, 2008. Refer endnote 7.

24 Mohlala, J., Goldman, G.A. and Goosen, X. 2012. Employee retention within the Information Technology division of a South African bank. *SA Journal of Human Resource Management*, 10(2), 1–11.

25 Allen, 2008. Refer endnote 7.

26 Gupta, A. and Tayal, T. (2013). Impact of competing force of motivational factors on employees at work place. *Information and Knowledge Management*, 3(5), 143–148.

27 Ramlall, 2004. Refer endnote 20.

28 Ramlall, 2004. Refer endnote 20.

29 Kinicki, A. and Fugate, M. 2012. *Organizational behaviour: Key concepts, skills and best practices* (5th ed.). New York: McGraw-Hill.

30 Paul and Berry, 2013. Refer endnote 16.

31 Ramlall, 2004. Refer endnote 20.

32 Castellano, S. 2013. Talent retention is a global challenge. *Training and Development*, 67(11), 18–19.

33 Fritz, J.H., O'Neil, N.B., Popp, A.M., Williams, C. and Arnett, R.C. 2012. The influence of supervisory behavioral integrity on intent to comply with organizational ethical standards and organizational commitment. *Journal of Business Ethics*, 114(2), 251–263.

34 WorldatWork. 2012. Refer to endnote 11.

35   Corporate Leadership Council. 2004. *Driving Performance and Retention through employee engagement – Executive Summary.* Retrieved from: https://www.stcloudstate.edu/humanresources/_files/documents/supv-brown-bag/employee-engagement.pdf

36   Cawe, M. 2006. *Factors contributing to employee engagement in South Africa.* Master's thesis. Faculty of Industrial Psychology and People Management, University of Johannesburg.

37   Gross, S.E. and Friedman, H.M. 2004. Creating an effective total reward strategy: Holistic approach supports business success. *Benefits Quarterly,* Third Quarter, 7-12.

38   Gross, S.E. and Friedman, H.M. 2007. *Creating an effective total rewards strategy: holistic approach better supports business success. Mercer Human Resources Consulting CD – Your guide to the age of talent.* New York: Mercer.

39   Torrington, D. & Torrington, D. 1931- 2009. *Fundamentals of human resource management: managing people at work* (1st ed.). New York: Prentice Hall/ Financial Times.

40   Bussin, M. 2017. The *Remuneration Handbook.* Bryanston: Knowledge Resources.

41   Bussin, 2017. Refer endnote 40.

42   Minchington, B. 2010. *Employer brand leadership: A global perspective.* Torrensville: Collective Learning Australia.

43   Corporate Leadership Council. 2007. *Leveraging Total Rewards to Attract and Retain In-Store employees.* Retrieved from: http://www.corporateleadershipcouncil.com.

44   Tandehill Human Capital. October, 2006. Total Rewards: The Employment Value Proposition. *Workspan Magazine.* Retrieved from: http://www.tandehill.com/pdfs/total-rewards.pdf

45   Lamoureux, K., Campbell, M., & Smith, R. April 2009. *High-impact succession management: Best practices, models and case studies in organizational talent mobility.* New York: Bersin & Associates and Center for Creative Leadership.

46   Towers Perrin. 2007. *Using total rewards to build an effective employee value proposition.* Retrieved from: http://www.towersperrin.com

47   Black, S. 2008. *The employee value proposition: how to be an employer of choice.* Retrieved from: http://www.knowledge.insead.edu.

48   Armstrong, M. & Brown, D. 2006. *Strategic reward: making it happen.* London: Kogan Page Publishers.

49   Hospitalityonline. 1998-2018. *Employer Profile.* Retrieved from: https://www.hospitalityonline.com/employers/231770

50   Corporate Leadership Council. 2007. New roadmap to engagement. *Business Wire.* Retrieved from: https://www.businesswire.com/news/home/20070411005813/en/Corporate-Leadership-Council-Identifies-New-Roadmap-Engagement

Index